This Is It, Coyote

Nancy Neithercut

Chapters

Dear Reader 5

Shadows In The Wind 9

Mirrored Glance Of No Tomorrow 30

Flowing Gown Of Mirrors 48

Ocean Swallows Itself 66

No Moon Empty Sky 83

Wind Paints Itself With Wind 93

Forest OF Sky 118

Carpet Of Moon 147

Echoes Have No Source 162

Liquid Eyes Of Love 190

Your Own Love Calls You Home 227

This Bird Sings 253

Dear Reader,

Imagine watching your hands crochet a lace skirt, watching your feet pad along a path, your voice singing, your thumb tapping songs on a glass screen and never feeling like there is a you doing or not doing anything or nothing.

Imagine the feeling that there are no separate things. No one thing being pummeled about by other things, like being in a universe of ping pong balls. No longer feeling like this is a universe filled with razor sharp edges that all feel like barriers between your broken heart and a love light you just know must be there somewhere.

Imagine knowing always that there is no other more better or next, that what seems to appear is indeed always it. Wouldn't there be a seamless ease and an unspeakable quietude no matter what seems to appear, when all hope and fear and need of a never arising next is gone?

Imagine no longer trying to change or fix yourself or others or the world, as you know without a doubt that life is, just as it seems to appear, utterly perfect.

Imagine knowing that no one, including you, is the instigator of their thought feeling or action, that life indeed does itself, totally spontaneously. Imagine knowing and feeling always that there are no separate things or feelings or thoughts or moments. That there is no right or wrong way to feel or think or act or live or love or die.

Imagine knowing you and everyone you love or have ever loved is a dream character in a play that no one wrote, that sings itself, that all measurement and dimension and time and love are made up. Imagine knowing that this life just as it seems to appear is the only life you can ever know, and there is no one who can escape.

Imagine knowing deeply that although love and beauty arise only in the dream through your beautiful eyes, and that there are no others, you can only see your imaginary reflection in this love dance with others.

Imagine that this vast emptiness you have tried to fill your entire life is true. That you are a flowing thought dream and are ultimately alone, yet here you are, most magically appearing, dancing in the grand canyon of love.

Some of these words will slide into boxes of the already known. Some may skip out of the grooves of habitual thought patterns and catapult you out of the assumption of knowing into an edgeless incertitude.

Shadows flicker and swirl across and through your feet your face your heart in this dance without a center or edge. Light and wind stream from everywhere from nowhere from inside and outside, there is no source to the echo that reverberates through your thought stream as you are not separate from it. You cannot find separate thoughts, separate feelings, separate moments, or anything truly to hold onto or any place to rest.

You are the looking for certitude, the fear of unknowing, the fear of disappearing in this love dance with which you long to merge. You cannot merge with it as you are it. You have never been separate from what's going on, this beautiful flow of life, this fleeting wind ballet that seems to embrace you and push and pull you along.

You are the pushing and pulling, the trying to hold it to capture it to make permanent this magic that you sense lies behind your shadow. But there is nothing painting your reflection, no one fills your shoes and sweeps you across the dance floor. There is no floor to stand on to dance on, to lie upon when you die.

You are the prism between the imaginary known and the unknowable, pouring color and light into the dream. Flooding the pages of your story with love and beauty that disappear the moment these words paint you. Just like this, as it has always been, yet never was, nor ever will be, you are this ever emerging ever wilting blooming flower of life feeling it's own tender vibrant aliveness through the symphony of perception and its inseparable recognition.

Painted with watercolor tears in the river of song, written with sky in sky, with your very breath and heartbeat, life sings you as you sing these very words within which you emerge.

You come to me with your methods and practices you believe will lead to a peaceful mind.
I say the quiescence of which I sing has nothing to do with if there are thoughts or not.
I do not see you as the instigator of thought feeling belief or action.
I feel your longing for this silence, this hush, that you believe your practice will give you.
You are this longing
And the hush
You cannot find it
Or create it anew.

All these teachers and teachings imply that they have something you do not.
That somehow you are flawed.
I do not see you as broken.
They imply that there is a destination and perpetuate the painful belief in other better more and next.
All there is is this edgeless sweeping momentary, you know that...

I see you as unspeakably beautiful no matter what you seem to believe or think.
And I weep that you cannot see this
No one can see their own beauty.

Come closer that we may bask in the beauty of each other's reflections... this imaginary space in-between us, the only place we exist.

I'm not here to help you or heal you. I cannot give you anything. Or nothing. I cannot share this sublime emptiness as there is no one who has it. I will not tell you more lies for you to weave into the wall of fear of unknowing that you are.

a tiny box of shells...a roomful of wind
acres of empty sky... refrigerator hum...
sound of the sea laughing

how I long to send you an empty bottle of wind you can sail into a
paper cup, and drink this wondrousness that paints me, dips its
brush into pools of echoes and swirls color, tears and blood
into a river
of reflections

Morning sleeps

Thought spins this night dream softly into day dream

Lyrical fluted transparent tapestries weaving and unweaving
themselves

Skimming and diving and soaring

Painting this shimmering aliveness

Edgeless colors melt into and through ephemeral swirling
iridescence

Searing brilliance of dawn

I am liquid eyes

And the waters

Flowing...

Utterly Amazing, beautiful you!

Love,
Nancy

Shadows In The Wind

Wet in wet
Blue in blue
Vastness in vastness
Sky in sky

Love wrote your name in the river and you could no longer find it,
you are the flowing the swirling the laughing the weeping. Not lost
nor found,
empty footfalls
empty handfuls of wind.

Day fades into your beautiful sunset
Colors bleeding
Sea and sky echo this last kiss

Voices of thought, bits of song, tendrils of memory untie themselves
in the wind. A crow dives and dances and lands in the tops of the
swaying palms. Ocean whispers, 'there is no time', and you
remember, as you are carried into this sensuousness of lostness.
Of the fullness of sky, and the death of grasping.
Only memory painted your reaching hands, your trembling heart
that ached for tomorrow and wept at the never forever beauty of
time.

Dissolved yet dancing
Longing of wind
Sings your name

Love wrote her name in the sea-foam clouds and she watched
them dissolve in the whirlpools and eddies of sky and the
fathomless suck of tides.
'Why me?', Why love?'

All questions fell through the deep abyss that closed when joy and sorrow merged and smiled.

I am as you see me
A girl a woman an artist a poet…
What is it that draws these hands that scribbles these lines that paints my mouth that sings these words that dance across your mind stream? What is it that longs to kiss a love song in your heart, your very own love song that sings you?

I am this longing this ache of never and forever that dances life into the looking glass and twirls.

I am a symphony of words falling through a song of unknowing.

What is enlightenment
What is a sage
What is the sound of moonlight shimmering on the receding waves

Rush and roar of traffic
Afternoon sun
Catches
One
Falling
Golden
Leaf

Falling mountain echo
Dissolves in the canyon
Love
A kiss of shadows
Streaming through each other
Always a perfect fit

Real
Unreal
This kiss of no tomorrow
From the inside

From the outside
Death dissolves all sides
Looking out
Looking in

Light pouring through light
Space into space
Emptiness into emptiness
No things to grasp
Leaves no grasper
Time an illusion
The morning glory sings

skin blood bones rocks
under the roots
more roots

mountain spills into the valley
words paint this song of empty shadows
that no one wears

Full moon
Tugs the tides
Tugs my heart
I cannot pluck its beauty from the shadows
No one can point to what is not
There are no empty hands
Or fingers pointing
Mystery another name to try to hold the ocean
That lies beneath this breath
Under the stillness
Not even nothing

Unadorned radiance
Blooms
We are the petals
Wilting

Supreme vast spaciousness
Without time or non time
Without space or emptiness
Without direction or non direction
Without movement or non movement
Without ending or beginning
Without emptiness or fullness.

There is no emptiness that can be filled,
Nor fullness that need be emptied.
Nothing need be done,
Nothing can be done.

There is no path and no one to follow,
No one to arrive and no goal to reach.
No ground and no one to fall.
No wisdom to attain,
Or ignorance to lose.
There is no one to be confused or non confused.
It cannot be grasped as you are not separate from it
There is no separation,
No separate things or events can be found.
Looking for it seems to push it away.
It is intuited and need not and cannot be understood.

Always on
Stillness

Weaving and unweaving the hem of her empty dress
Tattered dreams that no one wore
Strolling through the canyon of silent footfalls crumbling

Between everything and nothing tendrils of emptiness weave sound
into shadow, light into echoes that no one can find.
Beautifully woven light dreams of endless seas and edgeless skies
kiss as we sit on a fallen tree in the summer sun. I lost myself on
the path to nowhere and found us dancing down the timeless empty
streets of mind. Color and light and form seem to appear, yet they
are empty of meaning or non meaning.

She reached in the dark places where no one lived and found flowers in the dirt.
Growing towards the light and wilting in this empty love song that thrums thrums thrums through her heart. This is beautiful she whispered, to no one, to everyone, to her own reflection that has always been dancing with death. Drowned in your own darkness, love is finding you can breathe underwater.

Overtones and undertones reverberate into this heart song that sings itself. You can hear it always in the ease of life feeling it's own aliveness through you. Light and shadow need each other to twist and twine and flow through the embrace of never forever.
 Time, a beautiful day dream that gives you a seat on the train to your own demise. Knowing love is as real as tomorrow you find yourself weeping, how beautiful the sunset as it echoes your name.

Beauty a name for what seems to slaughter us with its very un-graspable impermanence. Yet we are the beauty, we are the dance twirling down the Grand Canyon of love.

All by itself life sings and dances a love song of one of two of many of none. How or why is no longer asked. It's the unknowing that whooshed into the whoosh and was recognized as the most precious jewel.

after the spring rains
where will you hide your heart
this floating world
butterflies hover
and vanish

The beauty of life just as it seems to appear
The uncaptureabilty
The unfigureoutability
The knowing of utter impermanence....
That life does itself
Effortless

It's the fluidity

The edgeless-ness
That wows

Lassos of sky cannot consume blue
Push and pull of tides
Naked cliffs
Wind and sun
Fall into the sea
Horizons never reached
Inside has no place
Outside no lines
Ever present all encompassing aliveness
Brief
Tenderness blossoms
Wilts and dies
Like the sun and wind
Tears and kisses on your cheeks
These words that fade as soon as they are spoken.
This life that dissolves as soon as it paints itself
Tears flow as a river into the edgeless sea

Ravishingly beautiful this beauty that cannot be captured with
words or hearts or minds

Sublimely beautiful how love, simply a word, is known and felt by
all, yet has no outlines or in-lines, and it is the line-less-ness we
love and recognize and feel so deeply.

The softness of no tomorrow
Slaughtered me with unbearable beauty
As though there were someone to let go…
or hold onto the day
She kissed the wind to find direction and felt the sea fall all around
her. There was no purchase on the starlit path. She wondered if her
feet were hers. There was no comfort in adding up a lifetime, no
rungs on the ladder of time. Vault of sky crashed and there was
nothing above.

First crow of morning had no meaning nor the sun's first warmth. Her heart collided with an echo of love, and dropped beneath the bottomless depths. Below time there was raw sublime aloneness.

Ocean song poured through her. Adrift on a sea of dreams, love had no place when it was everywhere. And nowhere. Only this song of love that had no source or goal or words that needed remembering. A reflection of futures day's past cast a lifetime of shadows across the skyline. It un-wrapped her nakedness with a story of a girl who lost herself and found these beautiful liquid eyes.

Ocean bathes
Wet in wet
Sun dances
Light in light
Wind surfs wind
Life breathes
Echoes play
Rippling reflections
Of reflections
Of reflections
Of reflections

Mirrored glance reveals
Starlight pouring through me
Through you
Ballet of time and place
Empty beyond empty
Full and rich beyond measure
We arise in the dance
The twining
Of shine and shadow
A caress a kiss a gesture a touch reveals an empty hand
Longing to be held

Wind blows and falls silent
Song of flowers blooming
Day grows and falls into its own hush

Love wrote her name in my heart

Moonlight swoons through moon-glow
She sings her name
our names
just like this

Where is yesterday's sky
Where are the tears of tomorrow
When is your heart
Not weeping

I see the footprint of my heart
Hanging in it's own shadow
Blossoming into golden
autumn leaves falling

I spied my shadow lingering on the garden path
Lustrous moon filled my footsteps
The empty dawn

what happens to this game of illusion when it's realized that no one
threw the dice and every number is magic? the edges of the dots
begin to blur...

So tender, so delicate, these rippling waters reflecting wetness in
wetness, light in light, simply sourceless echoes that illuminate your
tears.

Weeping
Not joy nor sorrow
Sublimely bittersweet
Tears reflect your naked heart

The feast is always on
Rarely noticed
Delicious beyond measure
Yet
Brief
That is one of life's tastiest parts

And then there is love...

The space between the lips and the kiss
Between the breath and the song
The hush the pause that is always on

Whispers of nothingness weave a web where jewels are caught in
moonlight

Cast adrift on an edgeless sea of dreams
Bottomless inky blackness below
Endless vault of sky above
Suns and moons flowing through you
The shimmering surface a reflection of your own gaze

His name, a crown, the prow of a ship born on a river of time.
Propelled by a tsunami of fear. Pulled by the call of a distant
horizon and a diamond see...

Cloud shadows soothed his naked desire to feel all the love he
feared to lose, but the swirling empty dresses parted in the clear
light of recognizing his hands had never steered this ship on a
shoreless ocean.

A shadow soared over the shimmering reflections and he looked
up, yet he could not find a cause nor trace of what had never been
and what would never be.
Like an unheard unsung song on the tip of his tongue, empty
verses lost their grip, and a kiss from within broke the silent sound
barrier between love and joy and sorrow and the ache for what
was.

Memories fell into the vastness as his ticket had no destination, his
dance card was unsigned. A brilliant vacancy, no name on the open
door, light streamed through the cracks in the ceiling and the floor
boards. Winds blew through his unfettered un feathered
nakedness.

Rains plummeted into vast unending sky as he was crushed by the
enormity of nothing left to do or say. No one left to do or say
anything or nothing. Simply this utter undeniable magnificent
enormity of light dancing.

His heart exploded from his empty chest and revealed the treasure
he had been searching for.

the empty gown swirls
and sings

Weeping and laughing deeply without line or tether, vast songs flow
weaving the dream into songs of lions roaring, of butterfly kisses
without nets. A touch less touch of midnight hush basks in its own
reflection.

He never needed to see where the sky kissed the sea, it was his
own moon rising in the unfathomable ocean of tears where he
drowned.

It all unwrites itself
like a tight knot
seemingly imperturbable
the loose ends
of emptiness
like tendrils of unbroken sky
un do themselves
Finding nothing underneath the wraps
most grab onto whatever description seems to fill the gaps
but its all gap...

The invisible man
there was really
really
really
nothing there

Last song of returning partygoers echoes into the sea. Waves crash and recede and reverberate up the cliffs. Symphony of night, of cricket song, the sleeping breath of morning, faucet slowly drips into a bucket, and the first crows call and answer. They weave their nests in the tops of the towering palms which sway outside our balcony. The heaviness of stillness whispering 'this is it' is evoked by poems that stir our hearts with a beautiful longing that cannot be caught.

And who would want to catch the morning breeze, or stop thought? They exist in their movement, this caress of life swirling. Life seems to dance all around you, yet without you there is no dance no wind no waves to sing of your aloneness. No one to revel in the intimacy of touching hearing watching tasting this all pervading feeling of aliveness that permeates the passion play. You are not separate from feeling, no one has it. You are not separate from thought, there is no thinker. There is no one who can step outside of this edgeless sea of dreams and manipulate the wind.

We are Impressions of reflections, a gossamer woven light raft shimmering on the see of dreams.

footprints dancing on the edge of time...

there was never a moon nor anyone to point
no time when or before or after

Hello goodbye hello this afternoon without time
Unending magic hour
Moonlight's shadow fills the cracks where I lost my reflection
infinite beauty ricocheting reverberating echoing

Infused with stories of love songs
A kiss from within perfumes the vast canyon where I once lived and yet remain
This memory of love is who I am

Beauty roars flows tip toes
Infinite petals bloom
Filling me emptying me

Without these clothes of nakedness
I cannot feel the magnificent ache of sky

Memories lost their grip
The knots loosed themselves
Where were the strings that held my heart
Where were the ropes that moonlight slid down
Where were the vines that held my innermost being from exploding

Inside fell through outside
In between collapsed into in between
Half way towards up
A million shades of sunlight
erased the illusion of shine and shadow
My heart dropped
weeping and laughing deeply at the same time
Water colors on the river
This ever blossoming ever wilting momentary emerging and
dissolving into itself sings

Tears flow
the world is weeping
slipping into the imaginary spaces between us
love ignites

Washed in ringlets of dew
set adrift
gossiping among the stars

Her reflection smiled back
Dreams of kisses unanswered
Tomorrow fell into a broken memory
A single leaf sailed unencumbered by its golden radiance
Leaving no mark to meter out time
The stillness of whirlpools singing of oceans vast
Never caught, the wet in wet

Infinite permutations of blue on blue on blue on blue
Vault of sky without end

An echo of a baby's cry sails across the sea
Abject aloneness reigns

Wet in wet in wet in wet
Weight of light through water
Sky flowers bloom
Sublime heartache of this fleeting kiss

this touch that finds itself only in the barriers that reflect your
mirrored glance
your beautiful beautiful eyes
weep

Love has already slaughtered you. Can you remember when you
first felt all alone? Can you remember when you didn't feel this
heartache?

Love has already shattered your heart into infinite pieces. You don't
have to wait. There is no next. Every mirrored shard longs to kiss
itself, yet they were never apart, and need not be glued together.
You need no fixing.
There is no seed deep within that will grow and flower. You already
are the most beautiful flower. This heartache, this longing is you.
Life kisses itself through your beautiful beautiful eyes and lips and
tears. Just like this.

There must be two imaginary mirrors for reflections of reflections to
dance
Through you I can recognize my beauty
Through this dance I know love

And even these words
Like infinite emptiness nothingness
Cannot be imagined

This essential emptiness is beyond any idea of empty. Not like there is a glass that was full and now it's empty.
There is no container of emptiness.
There is not something which has disappeared and now there is nothing.

There can be a feeling of no you nor everything nor nothing. A spacious vast expanse without lines or edges and simultaneously the knowing that you exist only as these imaginary lines.

There is no word for the feeling of vast seamless thing-less-ness that includes and contains all things.

It always feels like what ever seems to appear Is utterly naturally perfect. Knowing that perfection and non perfection are made up, just like me, how magnificent this dream of you of me of we.
The longing to share this, knowing it cannot, draws my echo in sky.
When I'm not singing of this that cannot be kissed with words, there is truly nothing, suspended as awe.

When we are born we cry out!
Reaching out your fingers drenched in your own tears painting water colors on this river.
All the emptiness poured away and ran into beautiful rivulets and pools and oceans of tears

and the sapphire and the blue are inseparable... empty words describing an indivisible edgeless-ness…
and leaves and wind simply dance...
wind has no idea from where it came... and does not care
leaves have no concern as to why they fall and swirl and call winter into the sky
singers have no care as to why they sing...
rivers have no concern as to their name, and with no purpose they so beautifully flow....
...and when the notion of personal volition falls away life becomes a beautiful effortless timeless indescribable flow…

Words
Like a film of iridescent oil
Create dragons breathing fire
Battles won and lost
Time lost itself
but passion plays on…
The cup is painted with delicate swirls that spin clouds into your drink
We drink deeply this life that drinks us…
This tiny window
This brief glance
It fills us and pours us out
Through us the universe recognizes it's own aliveness and sings.

Palm fronds bend and sway, reaching arching, falling, twisting and painting a fabric of sky. Light dances through this wind ballet and weaves the earth with shine and shadow. Where does the path end and your feet begin? When is the sunlight bathing your face separate from you? Where does it's warmth begin and end? On your skin? In your heart? When were you ever separate from this sensuous symphony of perception? When have you ever been separate from the recognition of it? When has your tremendous aliveness not been obvious through this unspeakable majesty of life recognizing it's aliveness through your tender delicate eyes?

The story of palms dancing and a lonely wanderer adrift on the shifting sands writes your feet into the picture and seems to paint separate footfalls and someone weeping. Yet it is always life singing all by itself, there is no effort required to feel.

It may seem like the story of you is so opaque it has blocked the recognition of this joy of aliveness, but the knowing of your supreme beauty has never been lost and cannot be gained, as the recognition of it is your story also. Simply obvious always, awareness is aware of being aware through this passion play, this brief beautiful window of the story of your life just as it is right now.

Leaf and flower patterns flow over and under my feet and into the dawn. Inside and outside dissolve as I revel in this sensuous beauty of morning that breathes me. Thought sings just like this and a singer emerges in the dreamscape.

The first beach crows announce the end of darkness so that they may fly with their shadows across the sea. A call and answer love song bequeathes the day with a ballet of light and shadow. Ripples of wavelets swim under over and through each other and reflect echoes upon echoes mirroring endless sky as they recede into diamond sand.
Where were the footprints of yesterday's tomorrow that beckoned with promises of love unending? They vanished in the flowering of the richness and fullness of simply life flowing without time yet always in time. Never a step missed or taken in this love dance of one of two of many of none.

dew on the morning glory
night of weeping is over
day greets itself
the void has no echo
no mourning song
missing the sea
is walking by the sea
longing for the shimmering waves as they dance
love is like this

The perfect poem
Got away before he could sing it
It pierced his beating heart
and sunk his dreams like zeppelins in the night

He tore up the empty pages and wept
Not realizing he
Was the rainbow fish
That got away

Washing my dying mother in the tub,
She loved the warmth and her favorite soap.
She was so skinny!
The next time I washed her in bed.
I never believed she would die.
Until she did.

In her drawer of intimate clothing
After she died
Hundreds of unused lick-on tattoos

Scattered voices, bits of song and laughter weave themselves into ocean song. Egrets fly home to roost, white wings and the mirroring sea catch the last light. Thin moon paints a door into the cricket night. Walking through shadows that echo on the cliffs, the sublime ache of aloneness sings like this. All eyes are alive with the singing of it. Even the wind that dances in the palm fingers paints it across this path. It is the song of our aliveness that we share in the shadowland, and it is the twining of songs that brightens into this searing love.

I greet you and weep at your broken hearted beauty, or is it mine I see reflected in your beautiful beautiful eyes? I can no longer tell and do not care as I am this shared humanness. We exist only as each other's echoes and there is no original song from which we spring. Not eternal nor temporary the tears of time fled long ago and I can only see and feel this kiss that sings my lines, this love that bleeds into the dream.

There are no waves nor ocean without you. Your brain paints distinction through this ever flowing thought stream. Through words the picture of endless blue. Through song the painting of you on the cliff breathless with this overwhelming beauty of life singing you. Without words this unsigned current of emotion drinks you and fills you. What erases the lines between joy and sorrow is not the absence of words, it is the end of belief in them.

Thought becomes most beautiful when it is known to paint the wind.

There are no footprints on the road to nowhere
Not even mine

Last crickets pierce wind withered sky
Mourning love songs
Hang from a branch
Falling petals
Old poems
Dying

Caught on feathers
White sea bird
My eyes follow the sunset
Beauty weeps at its own unfathomable nature
Through these eyes
Love sings and paints the wetness that sees it
A sage is a self much like other imaginary selves, but their brain
has had a profound shift in perspective. There is no longer the
belief in separation, or the feeling of it. The essential emptiness of
things and the holder of them is always obvious. There is an ever
present awe and joy that permeate the dream, as enlightenment is
the dream as well. This seamless sublime ease that the sage feels
is not the end of self or thingness, it's the knowing that all thingness
is made up.

Knowing you and me and love is made up is not the end of love.

Dawn looks at me and does not turn away.
I write love letters that I cannot send.
I sing verses that it cannot hear.
In this dance of light and shadow that trace my steps, my heart
song, my breath in the wind, I emerge. In these wild lines that burst
from love's fire where there was not even darkness, nor emptiness,
nor even a void, day brakes and sings.

Whispered stories
Shadows in the wind
Empty silhouette of sky
You may find yourself walking along a beach and start to wonder if
you're in the water or on the sand. You may turn around to see from

where your footsteps came, and find none. You may begin to find the sea falling into sky as the lines that separated down and up begin to blur and you may begin to feel dizzy.

You may lunge into a hut on the beach where others gather and tremble at the enormity of sky and light and the absence of any safe harbor. You may mouth their words of vastness
For awhile

But the longing may outweigh the fear of unknowing and you may find an unspeakable joy when this absence of handholds leaves you sobbing, as you watch your dreams of love and tomorrow burn in this all consuming conflagration.

Never and forever collide in this unfathomable namelessness where tears still flow, but there is no one weeping.

The empty moon inside your heart
Cannot hold light
Nor shadow

Dusk flowers in the shadowland
Wind beats on these tattered shutters
Dark cannot hide your emptiness
Nor your tears

Crow sits in her nest at the tippy top of the tall swaying palm. She has no thought stream to tell her the wind or the night or that she exists. We cannot see the inside of our skull or the workings of our neurons, yet boundless sky appears in the day and the night time dream. Through the thought stream the sensory symphony seems to have edges, lassos in the sky, cliffs and clouds and night and day seem to appear. Before and after write your story. But there is no before thought, as before is thought. All description paints the dream, there is truly no this or that without words. All we can know is this thought dream, as we are it. There is no escape, there is no outside to the dream, as inside and outside are the dream.

Many believe that enlightenment means the end of the dream. An escape from their humanness. This is not the end of you and me and we, this is not the end of sorrow. This is not the end of desire. This is the end of the feeling that desire is happening to a person. This is the end of the feeling that sadness is happening to a you. There is no longer any feeling that joy and sorrow and love and longing are separate.

What could possibly split the night into a call and answer love song but this magnificent thought stream?

The lack of belief in next slaughtered me. Viciously it erased the parameters of who I thought I was. Realizing there was nothing other than this ultimate perfection dancing itself, which I had always suspected, eviscerated me. I lost my smile my lips my teeth my tongue my skin my heartbeat my breath my life as I knew it and found myself again, ravaged and spit out on the shore where even love had walked away.

I got on my feet and ran into love again. The pyre burnt itself and out of the ashes a beautiful beautiful dream arises. However it seems to appear is always perfect, knowing there is no perfection or flaw.

Is it bliss is it love is it awe?
It is a beautiful longing for simply this. Life flowing all by itself. Amazed still after all these years. Wide eyed love.

Light and wind and love and life stream through me as me, as they always have, all ideas of grasping are gone. It's not that my hands are empty or they disappeared, there was never anyone to catch the wind. Only words streaming through the vastness, the lines and squiggles evaporate upon hearing themselves. No castle was built and there is none to crumble, just cloud dreams that whispered of a vastness that could not be seen. It is felt now always as I dance on the edge of a feather between love and nothing at all.

Supreme spaciousness of knowing no thingness drinks me as I pour it into a paper cup and watch the swirling songs that glisten on my lips.   this all pervading love that has no name nor number was always present, I just never noticed. The lines that felt like a prison have become transparent. And I the center-less jewel sparkling.

There is no one who can step outside of what's going on to accept it or reject it as the effort to accept it or reject it is what's going on.

Mirrored Glance of No Tomorrow

Shattered windshield
Bits of ribbon
Adorn the pavement.
Diamond dreams scattered like sunlight across the sea.
Mirrored glance
Of no tomorrow
Reflects your face, your eyes, these tears that were never yours.

Were you ever?
Are you now?
Ocean song reveals a lostness that cannot be found.
Is it everywhere?
Is it nowhere?
Where were you when time died?

beauty whispers,
'I love you'
Love sings,
'You're beautiful,
I am you.'
I am a ghost in this shadow dance. Afterimages of sky tossed into the sea.
Wind whipped shallows swallowed by fathomless depths have no light until these words appear and project love's memories across this scintillating horizon.
This vibrant immediacy, this undeniable aliveness has inebriated all thoughts of thus-ness and unfurled love's wings into the shadowland that paint this beautiful water color dreamscape through my eyes.
To be here
Yet not
The moon I swallowed long ago exploded into this symphony of water birds soaring into the last suns rays. Into the lovers walking alone and together, their silhouettes reflecting on the wet sand. The

beauty of love and love lost caresses a heart into beating rhythmless rhythms on this sea of dreams.

the sound and feel of her footsteps wove her shadowland dream flowing around an empty center...

I think everyone feels that there is magic
Somewhere
Vaguely remembered
Like a song you once sang but cannot find the words...
I just knew it was here
Right here
On the tip of my tongue
How I longed to taste it so!
But it was this, just as it seems to appear, this is the magic. It was me that was the beautiful jewel... center-less edge-less... never gone away simply not recognized...

wetness looks to gather the river and weeps at the sound of its own weeping

There is no river without you
Nor wetness nor flow
What is a river?
Is there anything under the words but more words just like this?
Isn't under a word?
Flowing description paints the dream of this and that and rivers and time and the soft wet longing of the river for the sea.

Life kisses itself through these very lips that sing of its wonder and majesty. You cannot see yourself as you are life's imaginary window to the dream, but you can listen to life singing itself and recognize your tremendous beauty.

All of this symphony of uninterrupted perception and its inseparable recognition is an obvious confirmation of your beautiful magical aliveness, no matter what it looks or feels like.

There is no one who becomes enlightened. Enlightenment is a total shift in perspective when it's known and felt always that there are no separate things or moments.
The dream of objectified separation is no longer believed.

There is no one who can step outside of what is going on and accept or reject it as the effort to accept or reject would be what's going on. This is a total ripping and shredding apart of all that you have held to be true about yourself and your world and all ideas of truth or meaning and anyone to have them.

The profound shift in perspective called enlightenment is the knowing feeling always that there are no separate things or moments. The dream of separation continues yet it is no longer believed. Not even disbelief is believed.

Trail of blood and tears mark an imaginary timeline between birth and death. Footfalls worn away by despair seem to create a lightness and a letting go, yet there was no one to let go and nothing to grasp.

We are nothing but echoes of mirrored reflections, there is no dance without a you and me.
We are the music the song the ache of dawn to greet the morning.
We are life's ecstatic love dance. Life swooning into and through itself through this passion play. It sings itself just like this...

Sometimes a sweet melancholia weaves itself into the dream
Like Christmas tinsel sparkling in a robins nest
Spring and winter melting
Bits of blue shells among the pine needles
Serene in the hush of summer
A broken heart your only tether
To a song that sang you long ago

Who need remember the song of morning? When did these hairs turn grey? To whom does the day happen? It sings itself for no one to no one, yet there seem to be footsteps in the sand.

I hear laughter in the distance and turn around, it is my own voice that echoes in the night. Starlight bathes these feet that go nowhere yet seem to dance to the song of midnight. Dawn paints itself with sunset and beckons my embrace yet there are no arms to hold the sky as wind and light stream through me as me.

I look ahead and see a huge blank where dreams used to paint a life and someone walking, someone dancing, someone loving, and someone dying.

Thought made of shared learned words seems to create things called awareness and perception. Without imaginary thingness there is no movement nor non movement. There is not even emptiness, nor nothing. This unspeakable fathomlessness of the knowing feeling that all thingness including you is made up is astounding. There is unending awe.

This is the profound shift in perspective called enlightenment. Knowing that aware-ing is aware of aware-ing through this streaming thought dream, this consensus conceptual overlay many call the dream of separation in which you and me and the color yellow seem to appear. We can never know what it overlays as it is not a that. There is no this or that outside of the dream. There is no outside to the dream as inside and outside are all dream stuff. All we can know is the dream as we are the dream. Some brains can somehow see that they are making up the dream of this and that, and the dream is never again believed. Yet it is seen and felt to be overwhelmingly marvelous, this imaginary thingness that includes color and sunsets and you and me to look at each other and say, 'I love you. You're beautiful'

We emerge in the meeting of the I's. I dissolve into your beauty, and sing.

My story must be continuously written with bits of memory and thoughts of future and opinions of this symphony, otherwise I cannot find myself or the imaginary time line I walk along from birth to death. No self or others or the rhythm of this or that seem to appear until I hear my heart dancing.

Everything must go
Even emptiness
Even love
Even nothing
All ideas of what you believe yourself and love and life to be are ripped to shreds.

I am this loving of love knowing that there is no love, nor me.
Yet all remains
There are no things, yet everything is included

Sound and silence are made up like you and me and love. Yet songs paint the morning and the first crow calling.

No one ever quite believes the dream of this and that, in imaginary things. There is always the feeling of something either not quite right or horribly wrong! As there is an intuited feeling that life is fluid, and it's only memories that seem to give life a bit of stability, a bit of a handhold on it, a bit of control. It is known, but maybe not acknowledged, that if we could really choose thought and emotion and action we would choose nicer fluffier ones, more gentle action, etc. so there is the belief in stability yet the feeling of whoosh, and that creates great unease.

What is the meaning of beauty?
What is the magic of love?
The moon fell half way up.
I saw its light reflect in your eyes.
There is no perfect love or love that is not perfect.

It is the un-catch-ability, the impermanence, the unknowing (all that we feared), that is so delicious. That there was no one to catch it and nothing to grasp was our greatest fear and the most amazing beauty.

Enlightenment hurts like hell!
Seekers really don't want this.

They just want a more peaceful self or a better one or an 'enlightened' self. There is no one that awakens and no one who sleeps. There is no one traveling a path to nowhere.
There is no self period.
Nor are there things.
We exist only as this consensus conceptual overlay, this net of jewels. We are spinning echoes without a center or source, of infinite facets ricocheting off of each others eyes.

I swoon into your beauty, knowing beauty and love and you and I are made up. Knowing we exist only as reflections, as holograms dancing in this imaginary space between us.

The edgeless singularity cannot be known yet edgeless-ness can be intuited and felt always. It feels like a beautiful slow love dance falling into and through itself.

Moonlight catches their long summer dresses sailing along the beach.
They lost the gods of their parents and gather to worship an orb of reflected light.
Sublime is their longing they are trying to erase.
Wondrous is this love they fear and long for.
It is always on this grace of life dancing itself, yet all ideas of it seem to hide it's recognition.
What are you without your fervent belief in love or god or source and the idea that you can become it?
Pale moon vainly sings through the mist
Reveals your desperate heart
Ghost dancing by the river
Autumn leaf
Winter wind
Naked trees reach for sky

Darkness never caught a shadow
Nor light
How could you be separate from your heart your tears your feet that dance to this song of earth and sky? Where is the line between a kiss and your lips that sing of love and love lost, as earth drinks you in and sky spits you out and you are forever swallowed by your

beautiful broken heart. It was never your tears never your smile never your heart never your love, simply life's longing that swooned into its own love that dance your reflection in sky.

Rolling thunder ocean sings my opening lines and signs my name to the day. Morning stretches it's toes into dawn erasing the deep silent ache of night. Cries of the first crow echo across the cliffs. This all pervading silence is the feeling that there are no handfuls of sky, and no hand, not even an empty one.

Just like this life does itself
Just like this love sings.

I never miss a chance to say I love you.

If you say this is it, there is the implication that there is a that. There is no this nor that nor both nor neither. 'What's going on', also makes this seem like a thing. What's going on includes thought about what's not going on. There are no things nor non things yet all and everything is included. Where else could it possibly be? There is no here nor there. There is no one big thing called oneness or wholeness that seems to be divided or split with thought. Without thought there is not even nothing. Not even emptiness. Not even love.
There are no words that can kiss this seamlessness I have longed to share since this profound shift in perspective. It feels like love like awe like stillness singing an ocean song that bestows utter perfection to the dream of separation. A flowing undercurrent of a continuous sublime union of what was never separate.

This cannot be taught or learned or transmitted, although many say they have had a glimpse while reading these words or watching a video of me twirling down the canyon. But these glimpses fade and were actually not caused, as there is no cause and effect, there are no separate events or moments. Life simply and most beautifully happens all by itself, just like enlightenment. One moment I was the belief in other better more and next, and suddenly the belief in separation dropped, along with the hope and terrible fear and angst of my impending doom.

Night fades
Dawn paints sky
Eyes open
Ears hear thunderous waves
Thoughts happen
Coloring in a dreamscape
Of orang-y light bathing the sea
Of vast endless sky
Of palms dancing in the wind
Of a you who sees and hears and feels this vibrant aliveness
And knows that it is beautiful.

We are a lens, a prism.
Nothing gazes out into nothing, and through us color alights on the
trembling wings of a dragon fly. We are reflections painting beauty
and love into the dream.

Fire breathing dragon swallows itself
Morning pours itself into the sea
Drinking it's color, drunk on daylight
Evening swirls and greets the sunset
Hello goodbye hello
Day into day
Night into night
Life has no map
No invitation to the dance
That sings you
That paints your color in the sea of dreams

Wind cannot hold onto itself
Rivers are their flowing
Mind, the thought stream that names itself
Seems to capture the day in bits of memory that bleed into a
person who laughs and weeps and longs for tomorrow.

But there is no tomorrow nor yesterday
Even now is a myth.

It's simply life dancing
All by itself.
Death it's silly grin
Painted on moonlight
Shines a searing beauty to your breath
Your heartbeat
This love that has no answer
Nor needs one
To love
Just like this
The song of life that sings you
Drinks you and
Pours you out

She was the weaving of rain and sun through a veil of tears, a center-less jewel flowing...

Like a shadow flowing through an empty glass you cannot drink it. It pulls you in and consumes you. You and I are ultimately not even nothing, yet here we are dancing through this mind stream, and I am smitten with your obvious beauty and am saddened you cannot see it.
Seems just about everyone is seeking something they feel is either out there or inside somewhere. Maybe in their heart or brain or maybe they want what they feel some Guru or teacher has. Perhaps they read something in a book that sounded good that promised more, a better way to live or feel or love. Most seem to want to feel peace or bliss or love unending. They want to escape certain feelings and desires, longing to end desire is desire is it not?

Maybe they want to feel that this is all there is and want to find a way to feel this, not recognizing that wanting to feel that way is what is.

How can a brain which believes the thought dream it's painting stop believing in it? No one knows how, there certainly is no why. Yet this does occur, and along with the belief of separation ending is the end of the belief of other better more and next.

The imaginary character that the thought stream produces certainly doesn't have anything to do with it, as a deep roaring river cannot change the mountain spring from which it came.

I am in India right now, and it is a hot bed of seekers. So many lost people come here and find a path that perpetuates the illusion of a path and someone on it and an ever receding goal to reach. I have no need to sing here, to tell them that there is no path to nowhere and that they will never get this, no one does. They are beautiful in their seeking. They are the seeking.

There never was a home nor a you to leave. Or return. Yet memory provides love's timeline and kisses you into the dance. Where are your feet you wonder, as you look back and see empty shadows racing towards a tomorrow that never came? Only a mountain of dreams piled higher and higher that never reached the sky, the infinite blue you longed for, all cloud castles melted into the sea. Seems is always the key word. Stories write themselves and it seems like there is a star to this movie, an inside and an outside. But there is no next, no tomorrow and no one to have one. Only words sailing through the mind stream, painting the wind.

Words crumple and die as soon as they are spoken. We are a flowing tone poem that ceases to appear when the song stops. Words dance wind and swaying palms, and lovers strolling hand in hand in moonlight. Shadows pool in the death of song and reveal that even nothing is description. Love, a beautiful song that seems to beat my heart and ply these very words onto this screen. But there is no trembling heart nor dance of love and sorrow without the song of this and that, the heartbeat of existence.

First light pours through the window yet the crows still sleep. Nestled in the tippy tops of the slender palms tilt a whirl-ing outside our porch. They have no song without us, no wind ruffles their feathers. The sun shines their iridescence so beautifully only in our eyes. We are the story the words the letters, sky formed messages tattered by the winds, the words that paint time and dimension and all measurement of what is not a thing until named.

There is no emptiness or source or god from which life springs. It sings itself and we seem to appear, dancing, in this sound and light show, colored always with sunset, death a beautiful shadow present in every precious breath.

She had no hands to hold the night.
Words cast a shadow across your brow and illuminate your tears.

The utter sweetness of life, simply this beautiful aliveness is revealed when all separation is realized and felt to be made up. The passion play continues as this recognition is also the conceptual overlay. All we can know are concepts as we are conceptual beings, yet this intuited unicity cannot be spoken of or pointed to as all words seem to divide what was never separate and was never a thing.

The shift is not a new belief or understanding or philosophy. It is more of a ripping away of all belief of what you are and all you believed to be true about the world, including ideas like truth and meaning and non meaning.

There are no things nor non things, no this nor that nor both nor neither, not one nor two not many nor none. What is not a what? When is up? How high is yellow? What time is it in outer space? Where does the mountain begin and the valley end? How can you have five fingers and a thumb? How deep and wide is the horizon? Can you pick it up and tie it around the sun?

Your brain paints a picture in that skull of yours and just like the characters in your night time dream you appear to dance in the day. But day and night are mere names, there is no light nor shadow without words. Nor you nor me nor love.

Where are yesterday's kisses?
Crumbled footsteps fading into the song of tomorrow.
Memories of love and love lost cannot plant a flag in the sea.
Ocean has no time yet you can feel it's rhythm in your heart.
It's song remembers you and all you've loved and dissolves your love letters in its infinite tears.

Am I gentle? Am I strong? Wind does not ask where it goes. Painted by flowing sands across the desert the vastness of empty dreams devastated my heart and opened a freeway of light of beyond measure. I found there was no one making these footsteps. Not even the wind, nor the ocean, nor endless sky that seared the last vestiges of a vacant silhouette, of any sense of solidity, have beckoned since that day that night that daydream swung through joy and sorrow. Sliding down endless rainbows and up the other side, life catapulted me into bleeding colors that leave no footprint.

I am an echo reverberating across the empty dunes. I am the dance of moonlight. I am the song of naked cliffs crumbling into the sea. No one left and no one followed yet the wind pirouettes the sand into imprints that fade as I walk along the narrow beach, bordered by the vastness of endless liquidity and a home where I once lived.
Seabird cries
Kissing sea and sky
There is no middle
Nor end
To aloneness
Or love

I was the longing to not feel separate from the swaying palms and endless sky...
How I longed to escape the skin I was living in
Until I realized the skin was the longing and there was nothing underneath.

Who would be free of themselves?
There is no self nor non self nor anyone to have one or not have one.

Most mistake description for understanding
But all things are created by words and can only be described by other words
This is the conceptual overlay
You also appear to arise in the thought stream
You are imagined
And that is unimaginable

Wind whips up the cliffs and sings a love song like no other.
'There is no next', she whispers and the crows echo a beautiful
lostness as you stand, in love, with the stark aloneness that this
death brings.
It is the death of everything
The death of nothing
The death of silence
And sound
The death of moonlight shimmering on the waves and the death of
ancient promises of tomorrow.
Where is that tightrope you balanced on as you peered into the
darkness, wondering how many sunsets you would gather? Now
the folds of your skirt and the lines on your face reflect the only
sunset the only breath the only heartbeat you will ever know. The
vast enormity and weight of this knowing erupts into a richness and
lushness and juiciness of life swirling through you, as you are the
dancing.

'There is no other', the ocean sings and crashes your dreams of
love on the rocky cliffs. You were the dream of love and next and
now you are the dream of unknowing.

Just like this your limbs move, your feet dance, your mind sails
paper lanterns in the sky.

I finished my drink and peered into the paper cup and saw the
tremendous emptiness of my own reflection. There was no joy nor
sorrow that I hungered for, only to sing of the echoless night that
had consumed me and bloomed into a love song like no other.

I can feel the rhythm of the night but there are no feet that dance,
it's only my heartbeat echoing in the stars. There is no tomorrow
when the sun will rise, yet it's everywhere and nowhere, always
rising always setting, always beginning always ending, never
beginning never ending. Time collided with timelessness, never and
forever slid through each other and left an empty shadow that
neither love nor moonlight can fill or erase.

There is no understanding how this emptiness dances, as there is not one without the other, yet both are felt simultaneously. The majesty of a life without direction or ground to stand on leaves a crumpled paper cup tumbling down the vacant street, a flower that shed its petals into my eyes.

You are the skylight between the bejeweled neuronal dance and the picture of infinite stars strewn across your mind stream. Ropes of braided light untie themselves revealing an echo of a day dream shimmering, dissolving in the summer sun. Like ancient songs of tears that left their footprints long ago in your heart and signed the wetness with your name, the lines and squiggles, the letters, the words, the signs and symbols leave no place to plant a tree. There is nothing to be known or unknown. Nothingness and spaciousness, even emptiness appear to have a place when there is a looking for the looker. Yet there will never be anything or nothing lost or found.

When the words cease there is not even nothing. There is no before words as before is a word. There is no outside to this virtual reality painted by thought as all words reference other words, even wordlessness is an imaginary reference point. There is no inside to this pseudo reality, this magicians tale, as inside and outside are mentally fabricated.

You are the imaginary center around which the rest of the dream of this and that swirls. There is no morning birdsong, no magical steam rising from your tea, no early sun streaming through this window ,this apparent window, this apparent point of view that is you, without thought.

We are the magic of the dream of separation which cannot be thought out of, as we are painted by thought. How wondrous when it's realized that without apparent separation aware-ing cannot be aware of aware-ing. Without imaginary thingness there is no you, or me, or golden sunlight caressing these very words as my thumb slides across this glass screen.

I don't care what you believe or think. Come here and sit, we can bask in each other's beautiful reflections. There is no such thing as an empty mirror. We are the shimmering light dancing in between. Without each other we don't exist, and that is truly beautiful.

What is this vastness this you sometimes feel? It it an emptiness, a fullness? Sometimes it slides in between the colors of a rainbow, when you look for the colors in last night's dream. When you see the endless vault of stars and feel yourself getting pulled... when you are stunned by the majesty of a sunset or the wide open sea. When you fall in love, that whoosh into a delicious unknowing. It can feel that your feet return to the ground and it leaves, but it has never left, this knowing of seamlessness, it merely seems hidden by the imaginary line between inside and outside. Between your tears and you. Between this longing and you. Joy and sorrow merge so beautifully. They were never separate.
Nor a you from them.

Do you paint the sky or does the sky paint you? Or is vast endless sky painted by your brain? There are rainbows in your night time dream too.

You may find yourself dissolving into sky and wind as they flow through you, but your feet have never left the ground. It's simply that there is no one walking or dancing or longing for that endless kiss.

You remain as a magical illusion, as this ache that has no name. Not love nor sorrow nor joy nor longing... yet a beautiful ache that is our shared humanness dancing

Drenched with starlight's song
Memories and the first bird
Day dream begins
Stretches it's toes onto the garden path
Seaside dew
Morning tears
Jewel laden petals

Echo the death of night
Reflect sky
Your tear stained cheeks
I weep

Always dawn
Always sunset
Always this kiss
Without another

No other
Or next
Endless sea
Ocean song
Child and oldster
I am both
And neither
Love
A player piano in the corner
Rippling
Drenched in wonder
Cascading ascending arpeggios
Have no words
Yet sing me
Sing you
Sing this love dance
To thee

Sea sighs and dreams you in its wind whipped waves.
Sky sings ancient love songs for the day.
Memories skip and sail across the mirrored waters as reflections
reach up to kiss the clouds that weep them, and are wrapped in
their own cascade.
Sea birds caught in sunset dissolve into the catapult of wonder that
erupted the day you realized there was no tomorrow.

There is no space between sky and it's sea mirror of blue in blue in
blue. Or between you and me, but there is where we dance.
Bathing in each other's reflections our imaginary lines form as they
dissolve, hello goodbye hello. We are love's echoes, can you hear

your heart, my heart, the hearts of many, of every tear stained shadow that has sailed the earth in its quest for completion?

You were never empty, you cannot be filled. There is no shadow that can be captured with its own light. Yet in the shadow lands love can reach in its hand and hold you in its dream time embrace, in this dream that rock and rolls you, in this dream of thought that paints you so beautifully through my eyes, I weep.

Love flows into itself and wilts all the blossoms you wanted for a bower. Slays you with its own magnificence, even as it reveals itself to be a dream. Just as you discovered your footfalls had always been empty you found the ultimate emptiness of all and everything.

She waltzed into the garden clothed in her flowered gown and dissolved into a sea of awe.

She has had free glimpses of the edgeless-ness and is in love with the majesty and mystery she feels. Believing she is separate from it she tries to capture it, explain it, put god in her pocket. She believes she has a choice and that there is a path to knowing, when it is the unknowing that is so delicious, and there is no path to nowhere. The mystery and wonder and majesty she seeks is the knowing that she is not separate from it.

No one has a mind
Mind, the thought stream, thinks you

The brain seems to split up what's going on into separate things and events using shared learned words and concepts (thought), and then seems to put them together again into pleasing patterns that can feel like a type of completion, or wholeness, or understanding. Yet what's going on was never split and cannot and need not be glued together with yet more thought.

When the thought stream is believed by the brain that thinks it, there is a feeling that there is a you to whom life, and all these separate feelings thoughts and events are happening. There is the belief that there is a someone in the center of the swirling thought dream, who can step outside of it and choose this or that, choose thought and feeling and action. yet it can be obvious that that rarely seems to work, and it hurts. It feels like a prison and there is a longing to escape this prison of thought.

When thought is no longer believed, it's like the prison of words that paints us becomes transparent and is seen as the most beautiful jewel in the universe.
You are that lens, that prism, that seems to create an inside and outside, a center-less jewel spinning...

The unraveling happens, just like all of life, all by itself. No one pulls the threads, you are the push pull of the tides, the flowing water, the wet of wet. Underneath the beautiful tapestry of belief there is not even nothing.
I am beliefs.
And that is a belief.
Belief and disbelief are no longer believed.
Simply flowing description painting the wind.

There is no self nor non self nor anyone to have or not have one.
Self is pretense but there is no one or thing that is pretending.
There is no pure consciousness or timeless awareness that either identifies with self or not.
There is no now nor anyone to be in it or out of it.

There is no enlightenment and no one to attain it. There is no other better more or next and no one to have it. There is no now and no one to be in it or out of it. There is no this nor that nor both nor neither, there are no things nor non things, yet everything is included.

The dream of separation is either believed or not by the brain that paints it. The consensus conceptual overlay, the world of this and that is the only world we, as conceptual beings, can know.

This is it coyote

Flowing Gown Of Mirrors

Footless shoes
Dance
In an empty room
Without a ceiling
Or floor
Or the walls that reflect their shadow.

Only ever this wave falling silently softly rushing roaring streaming soaring crashing into itself. Slipping into its own shadow in the dark moonlight. Only ever this breath this song this wonderment of light and shadow dancing with its own edgeless reflection.

Only ever this kiss, the first and last, this meeting of night and day where joy and sorrow paint a brief echo of your laughter and tears in seamless sky. Only ever this fleeting whisper of hello goodbye hello that sings you as you sing it. Love writes your name in a whirlpool and you watch your reflection appear and dissolve in the slip stream of thought. Only ever this day this night this timeless sliding into between and through the lines.

Only ever this collision of never and forever in this heartbeat this voice these lips this smile these tears shining sparkling, this ungraspable unfathomable majesty that falls in love with itself through your eyes.

the deafening song of midnight bloomed and swallowed her shadow
moonlight spilled into her paper heart
unfolding her fear of no tomorrow
Wings unfurled into the setting sun.

This dream time dance that sings her melancholy smile paints her footsteps with wind. Life flows through her as she is life dancing. A pirouetting silhouette of echoes, a billowing transparent gown of awe that no one is wearing, not even the sky.

No one pushes or pulls the tides, not a great intelligence nor god nor even the moon. No one or thing is outside of this life is animating it or making it happen. There is no edge to what is going on, it is not even an it. There are no edges that are not created by thought. The moon is painted not with reflected light, but with thought, and beauty is thought painting your beautiful beautiful eyes.

Echoes weave themselves into a surround sound dream scape of light and shadow dancing, light flowing through light, space falling through space and you wonder where you are in this vast unknowing. How exquisite when you lost your map your sextant your shadow as your footprints filled with stars?

You drowned in the wetness of wetness and found it was your own tears. You felt a feathered embrace and found it was your own wings, an inside outside embrace of life waltzing its ever present kiss of this and that into your heartbeat. All these words can never gather sunlight in your hand, yet they paint morphing sliding images with reflections of reflections, rippling iridescence flowing light and color and sound infolding unfolding blossoming into this dreamscape of you and your world.

How hauntingly beautiful we can only see our own beauty reflected in each other's eyes.

It seems you're having glimpses and they go away. You become the longing to have them return. It's shattering isn't it? All your ideas of what this looks and feels like, of other better more and next are being ripped apart. What would you be without these ideas?

The war ends
No one wins
No one loses
It was never about you

First I was the longing to not feel separate from the trees and wind and sky
Now I am the longing to share the deeply felt intuition of unicity
Knowing it cannot

We are our lines
The lines are imaginary

Imaginary separation, the jewel of the universe
All these infinite facets of nothing at all
Sparkling
Just so

A kaleidoscope of multifaceted jewelry weaving itself into tattered remnants of a shattered dreamscape washing in with the tides, sparkling in the summer sun as it percolates into the sandy beaches of this shoreless ocean, this sea of dreams, this mentally fabricated world, the only world we can know.

The symphony of perception, sight sound taste touch sensation feeling arises equally and evenly without any effort or non effort and is simultaneously inseparably recognized without any effort or non effort, without anything needing to be done. The thought stream describes it without any effort or non effort, without anything needing to be done.

The feeling of effort and the feeling of ease arise evenly and equally without any effort or non effort, without anything needing to be done. You know the life happens utterly spontaneously, all by itself.

Aware-ing is always on, it is not a thing as it is inseparable from the flow of perception, which is also not a thing. All thingness arises only in the description, the thought stream, that paints wind and tree tops dancing. You are this fleeting flowing description that seems to have solidity, yet does not. This fluidity and un-graspabilty you fear is the beauty and love you seek, but cannot hold. This delicious unknowing is the emptiness you sense, you cannot step into it or out of it, as it is right here in the taste of taste. The light of light, the fullness dancing.

I am a flowing gown of mirrors.
Reflections of reflections swimming over under and through themselves in this rippling sea of dreams.
Poems woven with light and shadow cannot kiss the land of no tomorrow.
They may resonate the heart strings of unknowing that seemed to tie up a vessel on an vacant shore. Your heart was always empty as it rippled with forgotten tales of wishes and regrets and sweet memories of love. Without this magicians tale there is no you to wander, no time to swoon into the dance that sings you. The sea has no harbor, no edge, where yesterday hides waiting for another kiss.

Signs and symbols words and letters spell this enchantment this song that we are. Hanging by moonbeams the morning rips the night and pulls the curtain off your slumber.

Where is yesterday's love where is that lonely street you wandered? Where is that river you crossed in last night's dream? Lost in the backbeat of memory like ancient footsteps on a forgotten path you can never trod again, you appear only in this shadow dance where never and forever collide.

There are no things nor non things
Not even nothing.
Not even emptiness exists.
Yet it is everywhere and nowhere
Extending infinitely without direction or center.
We cannot think or go beyond concepts, as we are thought, yet we can feel this vast spaciousness. It is not empty space that used to be or can be filled. When you reach the end of the known world, the conceptual reality, you realize there is no outside nor inside nor anyone to leave or return.

It's breathtakingly wondrous and utterly devastating to recognize the essential emptiness of thingness, as you are one of those apparent separate things.

There are no words that can kiss this sublime unknowing, that permeates the dream after the unraveling of every tattered fragment of you and your world.

There is no one or thing that remains stable, like self or true self or awareness or pure consciousness or god or source or emptiness. Not even love. Not one pretending to be two.
There is no one nor two, nor many nor none.

All these words simply are the dream of separation painting itself. All description is the dream unfolding unending blossoms of wonderment. Paper airplanes carrying messages that will never be read. As the origami sun unfolds into the sea reds and oranges paint the sea and sky, and the horizon slides into the empty page of night. There never was a tomorrow nor a you to greet it, yet here we are dancing on the edge of everything and nothing, just like this, life sings itself.

Wading through the words of sunset that paint colors and a sky and a reflection of someone to be enchanted. Footprints in the sand suggest a yesterday and tomorrow, yet they are simply memories that seem to form someone walking towards death on this magical timeline of sorrow and joy. Waves falling into and through themselves
Wet in wet
Starlight through starlight.
Imaginings of images of someone to greet the sunrise pull the tides around you when it's realized there is no day or night or time outside the thought dream that paints you and your tears. What magical illusion to know this is illusion.

I see your face and your shining beauty slow dancing through the windy night.

There is a deep deep beautiful melancholy I feel when I know you can never see it your own beauty. Only through your eyes can I see mine.
Only through this dance of reflections can I know love.

Such sublime rawness of an unprotected unowned heart.

Life expressing itself with these lips these teeth this smile this mouth that sings, these eyes that see and weep at the beauty of simply seeing. Simply the marvel of aliveness of just being, that blows light into the shadows and kisses you on the mouth and plunges it's heart into yours. Just like this, it has always been this way, we just never noticed.

Love softly calls your name in a whirlpool of echoes, in a bucket of stars, in the silence of midnight peeking through a warm summer's day. Ripping through the paint by numbers canvass that stretched your childhood dreams, casting shadows on your sunset, pronouncing syllables you cannot place yet recognize like an ancient language that need not be deciphered. A primordial song beckons you and you cannot turn away from its fiery kiss.

Oceans fall through oceans in this collision of sea and sky and sunsets, eating up all hope of the morrow or when this storm will end. Bereft of light and shadow there is no hand to grasp the tiller, no sails to catch the wind, no center to your sorrow, no edge to your joy. Melting into this unknowing that swallows you as you drink deeply this awe. Such unfathomable beauty that skims lightly over the sea and floods the waves and ripples with a searing light so brilliant so immense so overwhelming that you collapse into yourself and weep.

The sea left no footprints, nor the sky, nor the ashes of tomorrow that the wind absorbed in its effortless embrace.
Shimmering pools of star shadows adorn the vacant streets where you wandered for decades seeking the source of light. Certain to find an everlasting kiss, a vault of sky, some thing you could grasp and say, this is me, this is who I am.

You discover there is not even a thing called awareness or emptiness under the light. You panic and scramble for even more words to fill in the blanks to feed that gaping maw of desire to understand, to stop the dam of tears that would ensue when even zero won't keep your equation from collapsing.

There are no words numbers or symbols that do not reference other words. The universe is in the dictionary but you cannot drink it's waters nor sail it's seas nor feel it's tears on your beautiful cheeks. Under the garb of words there is no permanent unchanging you.

Love is in the dictionary...
What happens when the pages become unbound and winter blows away the crumbled leaves…

Here I cannot ignore the shift
EVER
It's so screamingly obvious
It wakes me in the morning and kisses me to sleep at night.
These futile attempts to kiss it, these poems sing me.

Wind dances in a spider web hung with jewels of sunset
Echos of dusk
Begin to pool
Beneath the steep cliffs
Crows start their evening song
Swooping into the towering palms for sleep

Who awaits the night of non remembering?
Who longs for a dawn that will not come?
Shadows swim through shadows looking for the light that will erase them
They never were

No one made these footsteps that crumble in the wind

Smile of moon hangs in twilight
Empty yet full
suspended in the pause
A promise of no tomorrow

Morning blooms as one unopened bud falls into the softness of yesterday's petals. Tides recede revealing your tattooed necklace of tears, a be-jeweled raiment of reflections, of ancient echoes softly flowing around and through an empty center. Fathomless depths fell up and swallowed endless sky, blue in blue in blue in blue, shimmering through the inky blackness that kissed you fully, deeper than your secret wishes. Wet in wet in wet in wet, leaving not even a sign to direct your feet or light for your eyes to follow in this map-less land that has no edges, no place to land, nor heart to long for it.

Not even nothing cannot fold itself into an empty paper cup or leave its calling card on the mantle. Yet on the rim of this empty vessel there is a shimmering brightness that sings your name so sweetly you find yourself drinking deeply again, nourished by your own love. Gone and returned instantly, you fell into and through yourself, eyes all aglow with the secret of secrets...
that all you longed to escape and your longing is the most beautiful story of all.

The stars need no map and their light needs no compass as it shimmers so delicately on the puddles left by last night's rain. There was never anything hidden under your shadow as it slid along the pavement in front of you in the empty streets of midnight. You cannot erase it as you dance with the night. The light in your eyes is only the moon's reflection. Not even love is hidden in the shadows waiting to dance. Lit from nowhere and everywhere, placeless-ness is revealed in the death of a thousand wishes.
Moving your feet, your eyes, your heart, under your smile, under your tears, under your skin, under your flowing gown of moonlight there is not even a sigh.

Last lily opens
Drinking hot chocolate
memories of love
Sing these lines
My lines
Dance a line between light and shadow

Sea foam clouds catch a glimpse of their own sparkling reflection
and percolate into the sands of the receding waves.

Shimmering rainbows inside the shell fade as my tears dry, weaving
a song of mournful beauty into the fabric of the dream.

Wind twisted pines bow to the sliver of moon as it greets its
reflection and dissolves into the sea.
A thousand sorrows fall into the hush of ocean night.

Life has plunged its reckless beauty into your heart and there is no
turning away from the gaping maw of the unfathomable emptiness
that is devouring you.

Towers of echoes
Walls of reflections
Light filled afterimages swirl
Dream castles of memories
Stairways to imagined futures
Ascending and descending arpeggios of sound
Waves crashing
Tides coming in and going out in endless sea
Without a shore to walk on
There is no wanderer
Without a song
There is no singer
Without a lover
There is no love

After the war
No one won
No one lost

They met on the blood soaked flowered fields
And warmed themselves in each other's sun
And drank deeply the refreshing coolness of each other's shade.

Sharing songs of passion and fury
And the all pervading stillness that floods earth and sky.

In love as love through love.
This dance of one of two of many
Of none

No light in the early morning village
Crows begin their song
I have my phone and poems start pouring
Hello goodbye hello

She longed for moonlight to dance her away…
She longed to merge with sea and sky
She longed to escape her longing
And found she was it

When the walls became transparent
She saw herself in everyone's eyes.
The death of tomorrow filled her, joy and sorrow sang an
indescribable sweetness.
A rich and lush searing brilliance lighting the dream that lights itself.
Within and without beautiful fabrications
These sourceless echoes
These baseless shimmering reflections need an imaginary center
To dance
An infinitely arrayed seamless vastness
Sings
Prism of thought
The lens between inside and out
This and that
The heartbeat of the dream

Morning sings
Golden waves dancing
Rocky cliffs by the sea
Rosy light in long autumn grasses
Paints my hand
My breath
My heartbeat
My feet
Wandering along the path
Footsteps in the sand
Tell a story of someone going somewhere
Nowhere
Everywhere
The thought dream dances
All encompassing edgeless vastness fills me
Emptiness me
Endless spaciousness blooming without time or non time

Swirling mirrored gypsy skirt
I am this empty shimmering raiment of reflections painting this song
and a singer

Soundless echoes slide through each other
Reverberating songs of placeless-ness falling through day and
night and time itself
symphony of rain sparkles
Sunlight in your smile

You wrote your story in the river
You tried to erase yourself
You saw your reflection flowing through you
Wet in wet in wet in wet
Your story
a water color dreamscape
Needs its banks to flow

Suspended
Without movement or non movement
Edgeless
Without direction or non direction

Life kissed you back into its embrace
As you embraced it
You found another looking through the mirror
And sang

A wave falling into and through itself
A sublime kiss of wind in wind

Even as small kids my brother and I would sing sad songs about
the loss of youth and the loss of love
And cry.
It seems as soon as the belief in the dream starts to kick in there
emerges a wistful sublime sadness of the preciousness of life and
love, just as that feeling of no separation starts to slip away

We are this beautiful achy break-y heart.

I was the longing to not feel separate from the wind dancing in the
tree tops. Now I'm the longing to share this feeling of seamless
ease.
Knowing it can never be shared is sublime. To know that I exist only
as an imaginary self and that self is desire.

Being suspended as nothingness
Is nothing to write home about.
The longing is most beautiful
It is who we are.

Along with the belief in separation there is the FEELING of
separation. A separate someone in a world of separate things and
events.
Thought that creates the conceptual reality of this and that when
believed by the brain that paints it feels wrong somehow, so many
try to get rid of or change thought or accept it to arrive at the peace
they imagine a sage lives in. But there is no one separate from
thought that can do or not do anything or nothing, as selves are an
imaginary product of the thought stream. All trying to do or not do
anything or nothing simply perpetuates the most painful illusion of a

separate self who can step outside of what is going on and manipulate it or accept or reject or surrender to it. There are no its nor whats nor whens.

It's obvious that with the belief in separation present there would be the belief that if there is thought, there is a thinker. If there are feelings, there is a feeler. If the universe seems intelligent, there is a god or consciousness or something making life happen. It's inconceivable that life happens all by itself.

If that is realized, there is always a seamless ease, a sublime quiescence that permeates the dream, as enlightenment is the dream as well. There is no requirement to erase thought or sound to recognize this silence of which I sing. There are no requirements whatsoever as enlightenment is utterly uncaused. It is not circumstantial. Just like life, awakening happens all by itself.

It requires imaginary separation in order to recognize this unicity that has no name or non name. The dream continues much as before. It's never believed. It never feels like life or thought or feeling is happening to a sage, or that there is someone doing it. imaginary division is no longer FELT.

Windless night
Steals the hush
From my breath
Sucks out the marrow
Of moon
And shadow
No footsteps to be empty or full
No path of stars to beckon
No song to call or answer

No sadness to weep at its own beauty
No laughter to ripple light into the darkness
No lovers to meet on the edge of midnight

When is the sound of moonlight?
Where is the wake of love?
What is this dance that consumes earth and sky?

Why this ache for nameless beauty?

You find yourself again
All questions dissolved in this searing brilliance that swallowed
even the sun
Dancing with your shadow on the windy cliffs
In love with the love of no tomorrow

It hurts like hell when the illusion of self and others is ripped to
shreds, as you are that illusion of separation.

I woke this morning, words swirling trying to kiss this infinite
intimate kiss of never and forever. I am this beautiful longing. The
kiss of inside and outside pierced me and I emerged as this
sublime ache of love of joy of sorrow of awe, this flowing
dreamscape of a heart that exploded and imploded.
These songs sing me, I only appear to mouth the words.

Whose words
Whose tears
Whose smile and laughter
Whose love
I do not know, and no longer try to capture the sky

When we look for what's looking and find not even nothing, it is
devastatingly ravishingly beautiful. Yet the concepts of emptiness
and nothing and awareness can fill in the blanks. Sometimes
temporary place holders remain. Sometimes they dissolve along
with the hand that grasped. Knowing that there are no reference
points whatsoever still there is dancing, but it never feels like there
is a dancer after the dance floor falls away. It feels like an ecstatic
love dance in love as love through love. Life singing you as you find
your mouth your lips your teeth your song this song of life of joy and
sorrow dancing through you as you.

Full moon exploded my empty heart
I crashed into the fullness

Of wetness
Of light
Of yellow flowers blooming on the banks of no tomorrow

River of dawn plays in the waves
Of the oceans remembering
Song of wind fills
An empty brush
Paints color and light
Life slides across the pages
Love bleeds into the paper
Tears saturate the fibers
Shred your being into
Ripples of memories
Sailing through moonlight

This unfathomable aliveness
That you are
Sings and knows it's singing

There is no truth nor anyone to have it. There is no enlightenment
nor anyone to get it. Yet the flowing thought dream that is the story
of you may begin to feel less solid, as the belief in and longing for
surety, as the belief in separation, the belief in begins to unravel.
The sextant starts to dissolve as the stars start to fall around and
through you. You cannot find your hand, your feet, your heart drops.
Most run for cover as the wall of fear of unknowing is quickly rebuilt
with old or new beliefs in god or awareness or true self fill in the
vast empty maw that is consuming you. But this meatless bone
may not be enough to fill that emptiness you feel inside...

Stepping lightly into the dream loosely wrapped as nakedness and
desire knowing these flowing mirrored garments are empty.
Transparent reflections dancing, life streaming through me as me.

Poems write me.
Shimmering lines fading in the mist.
Cliffs appear diving into the waves. Sea calls and answers its own
echoing brilliance. Songs erupt like morning from my chest. This
aliveness this hyper awareness of being aware is gently or

screamingly obvious always. So bittersweetly beautiful that it cannot be shared, and that there is no one with whom to share it.

The one who seems to hold onto illusion is illusion. Illusion is illusion.
You cannot allow thought and feeling to be as they are, as there is no thinker nor a feeler. You cannot allow or accept or reject or surrender to what's going on, as you are not separate from it. What's going on becomes the trying to allow it.
ALL trying or trying to not try perpetuates the painful illusion of separation. Doing nothing is also doing.

There is no one or thing that is experiencing thought feeling or sensation. Not even awareness or clarity or open intelligence.

All I can find, is the seamless uninterrupted symphony of perception and the simultaneous inseparable recognition of it. Only in the description made of shared learned words does it seem that there is a thing called experience and a someone or thing experiencing it. There are no its or things. No separate thoughts or feelings or emotions.
This is it coyote, whatever it looks or feels like.

We are center-less jewels radiating infinite mirrored reflections spinning a tale of love.

When the timeline from birth to death collapses
Those old shoes keep a-walk-in
No one wears them
They know how to dance

Ocean song beckons with the liquid embrace of no tomorrow.
Death of dreams another dream that no one would wish for.
Cascading love songs tear the curtain of belief in love.
Always this obvious scintillating vibrant aliveness, life touching seeing feeling it's own aliveness through the beautiful transparent prism of your eyes.

Mirrors exist only as their reflections.
Silence has no song without wind.
There are no edges that can contain nothing.
Without seekers a sage has no song.

He kept running up the cliffs trying to get above the horizon. Its
Impossible and tiresome to erase your story as the attempt to
erase it writes it.

Blown away by not even wind
Shimmering diamonds surfing your eyes
Sea slides into its own brilliance
Kissing sky
You are this song of beauty
Exploding from your chest.

She wore the thought of almost meeting
Steam curling from her morning tea

Mists of memory sailing without a port
Tears drowning in their own wetness
Wings unfurling in the hush of wind
Colors blooming in the song of midnight
And she danced a wildness that laughed and wept revealing your
rainbow reflection in her eyes
You fell through your nakedness
Astounded at the simple joy and beauty of your aliveness.

I was not sure what I had been seeking, not meaning or truth or
enlightenment, yet at the end of a lifetime of seeking, there was a
deep longing to not feel separate from the wind and tree tops
dancing. The grasping, searching for this always seemed to chase
it away. After a devastating ripping and shedding of all I had
considered to be true about myself and the world, including all
ideas of truth and meaning and anyone to have a world, there was
a profound shift in perspective.

This profound permanent shift is always radically obvious. There is no doubt that this is what the sages I had been reading were singing of, and no doubt that some of them had not seen it. There was no need of confirmation, and it has never gone away.

It is the end of belief in separation, yet the dream of separation, the conceptual virtual reality continues much as before. It is not an escape from the dream, nor from your beautiful humanness. I am still constantly amazed that all thingness is made up... even love is the dream, the best part of the song.

It's realized that the wondrous gem of imaginary separation is required for aware-ing to be aware of aware-ing. It's not about getting more or better awareness, as awareness is not a thing. It's not about achieving a rare goal or attaining a special gem. You already are that marvelous jewel, you cannot have it or hold it. It is center-less and edgeless. You can never find it hiding in these words as words create things and there are none. But it is always on, simply noticed or not.

Ocean Swallows Itself

Morning light listens
As night falls asleep
On my bed
In the garden
Nestling in dreams of sleep
The forgotten almost remembered
whispers what you fear
Yet long to hear
This is your only breath

Moon
An incessant traveler
Time sails for no one

First crow
Wind rustles the dead leaves outside my window

Thundering silence
Waves goodbye to autumn
A sonorous reflection of an echo seems to desire to listen...
To its own song
We are the longing that pulls us along

Under the name
Not even a shadow
A pause
Shot through itself
Completing a circle
That was never drawn

Night sleeps in the garden
Nestled in the leaves of darkness
Starlight dreams
Wind brushes the petals of longing
Turning tossing
Rippling over and under and through each other

Reflections of yesterday's mirrors
Pull and push
Night into day
Day into night
A breath
A heartbeat
Rustles the leaves
Write and erase my footsteps in sand

Colors bleed without your breath to burn the embers of time
Wind dies without your lips to kiss the words
Water has no wetness
Taste has no taste
Love has no love
Without your song
Singing you
The ocean swallows itself

First crow
starlit dawn
empty cliff path
Leads to the sunrise
Long yellow flowers in the wind

Poems sing me into the morning

Unraveled by her own love
Kissed again into the love dance
We know this love that pulls us along
We are it
No words for this love
Yet love is a word

Longing for what is
Includes longing

What whispered your name in the dark moonlight
Sideways glance
Reveals no singer

Morning glory
The hush of dawn
Stretch your toes into the day time dream

The uninterrupted symphony of perception and the inseparable
recognition of it is rich and lush. Only a tiny bit of it is described
named and known. Knowing description paints this dream we
share, yet not believing it, there is simply a noticing of the beauty of
the cracks in the asphalt while I'm driving in the obsidian night. Yet I
never seem to wander outside of the lines. They are me.

No longer trying to escape knowing there is no outside or inside,
nor before or after, there is a beautiful seamless ease that
permeates the dream.

As soon as imaginary separation is believed it feels like you've
been kicked out from heaven. When we fall in love it feels like the
doors of heaven are opening.

When it's realized that there are no things to be separate, it's like
the wings of heaven have unfolded inside and outside, and it's
known there was never a door nor a you to leave or enter.

Kali has no choice but to mirror your beautiful desire to be pierced
by love's heart magic. The mirror shatters and every shard reflects
your own love as it ravishes and eviscerates all ideas of love and
anyone to hold it.

I'm just watching the dancing shadows in the sink as my hands
wash themselves. As my friend talks about her day I am enchanted

with her beauty. Her voice is the wind and waves. The evening light streams through her hair and I feel like weeping.

Unending parentheses reverberating outwards and inwards, flowing ripples of space crossing over and under each other weaving a self illumined bejeweled fabric of echoes of echoes of echoes…

Night in day, day in night, the evening breeze flows through the canyon. Not longing for the dark or dawn the moon Lilly blooms. Sometimes the moon sails her petals into my heart and they bloom on this light screen. My thumb tapping the color of love into the dream.

Old stone walkway
Cows in the empty flower market
We watch them stand

One faltering street lamp
Sound of midnight
Listens to the flowers blooming

Nothing was bound by these ropes
Not even the sky

Ancient river
Rusty temple bells
wind sings

Wordless waves
Cliffside lodging
Slides into the sea

Forever collapses into never
Breath of moonlight

Come a little closer
What did you say?

I cannot hear your words
I am melting into your beauty

Raw and naked with nothing under your nakedness. Utterly
fearless, and hopeless.
No one to protect. Nothing to hide and no where to hide it.
We feel everything more deeply, feelings are not owned they are
everyone's, they are not happening TO someone. Some one yells
at me and I weep at the pain they feel, yet it is burned as it appears
as there is no where for it to lodge, all the secret pockets have been
ripped inside out. It is a beautiful life, this life of utter hopelessly
wondrous awe.

No bridge between here and there
Between you and I
Between yesterday and tomorrow
It collapsed when you tried to cross it
Day dreams crumble into night
Tree frogs sing

I am the longing for what is. The preciousness and tenuousness of
life. Looking and feeling like anything at all.

Long afternoon of summer
lanterned petals waving
Sunset kisses your tender cheek
This precious ache of no tomorrow

Rocked in the cradle of moon glow
Morning sings

Day unfolds into itself
Light has no weight
Time turns around and looks at itself

I hear my voice murmuring in the distance

I look for my footsteps
The edges of my song
My breath is the wind
That scattered them

She wandered the beaches looking for one smooth stone that
would match the one in her pocket. Wind blew the tops of the
waves backwards, laughing, swirling sand in her footsteps. Endless
ocean swallowed it's sandy shore. Endless sky fell into itself. She
lost all ideas of direction in the sound of sea. Ideas of a perfect love
crumbled as she discovered her aloneness. Stark yet beautiful time
dissolved into itself. As the dawn rose on an empty beach she
found herself walking.

Silence

Shimmering sea
Reflections singing sky

Transparency of light
Weighs down the night
We are the remembering

Trails of stars fell into this dream
Love lost it's shadow
In the empty dawn

Love planted it's poem in the halls of no tomorrow
A weight of words that could not be heard
Nor sung
Listening for the dawn
Sorrow it's own emptiness

He stood on the distant shore
Waiting for his echo
He peered into the looking
Folding into and through himself
Missives of love unanswered
Garlands of marigolds washing up in the sand

The words and responses that flow through me are not intended to make you feel comfortable or give you an anchor in the dream. They may trip up your ordinary thought patterns and leave you spinning, your mind hanging with no where to go. No handholds ...on a gangplank. Most will run for cover to the usual haunts of their old spiritual teachers and practices. After all, there is safety in numbers, isn't there? One million burgers sold. What would you do, where would you be, what would you be if there was no you nor place to land? What would you be without this imaginary certainty? Is there really anything solid stable and fixed? Is there really a constant permanent you separate and apart from what's going on?

All these decades of looking for peace or love or enlightenment... have they ever really brought you what you wanted? Do you really know what you want? If you knew it, you wouldn't be looking for it, would you?

With no separate moments there is no next. No one to fall or arise. Appear or disappear.
I am always here yet not as if walking as a dream and knowing it. Dancing in on the edge of a feather between everything and nothing, between love and nothing at all. Poems flood through me and write me and erase me, fill me and empty me, create me and vanquish me.

Love is a thing
And there are no things
Yet here we are
Loving each other
The effort to escape the dream paints a you into it. There is no shield between you and love or sorrow. How can you remove the wetness from your tears?

Where is the love in love?
The wetness of wet?
The taste of taste?

The looking for what's looking buries mirrors in the sands of sorrow.

As hope drowns in the sea's reflection, an amazing lightness is born.

Dancing on the edge of memory
Surrounded by darkness
No where to go but death

This vibrant aliveness you feel always is the magic that you are. Life touching, feeling it's own aliveness through you.

This miraculous aware-ing of being aware is always obvious as you emerge in the flames of thought. This fire that burns in your heart is the light of the world. This jewel of the universe that you are is the lens between the physical world and the imaginary. Life sings itself through your lips as you are the font of beauty in the sunset and love in the world. Who could ask for more?

Where is the space between two people laughing? Where is the space between two people weeping?

How close can I get with these words? How far is near? Where is the horizon between here and there? The lines and squiggles of these letters these words these thoughts that paint the sky weeping, never really divide the page into pieces. Never really sail across the paper maché moon. Only an origami boat made of tears can drown, like you with your crumpled books, so tired of looking for your face and who made it. Behind the mirror there was nothing, not even silence.
These poems form my bones and sing my teeth and lips and tears and claws.

Many teachers have bamboozled countless people into believing that there is a thing called now. This perpetuates the most painful illusion that there is a thing called you separate and apart from what's going on, and that this imaginary self can do or can not do anything or nothing to somehow accept or allow or surrender to a flow when all there is, is this edgeless seamless flow. An imaginary piece of sky cannot manipulate or join together the rest of sky.

Can you find the beginning and ending to a moment? When do they happen? When the clock ticks? What if there's no clock? What time is it on the sun? Are there really separate moments? Is there ever a you separate from what's going on? You cannot pinpoint time as you are a mental fabrication like time. If you feel like you are separate from what's going on, then that's what's going on.

Is there an edge or outside to what's going on? If there's no outside, there's no inside. You cannot capture something which is not separate from you. What's going on is not a thing, it cannot be grasped. You cannot step outside of it and manipulate or accept or reject or surrender to this edgeless uninterrupted flow. Trying to allow or accept or reject or surrender to it, is it, and it's not an it.

We can only know or see imaginary thingness. There are no words for what cannot be named, yet I just named it and seemed to create a thing.
All words seem to create things and there are none.

Just like this the dream paints itself... hands reaching in the dark for light find their fingers and the wetness of tears when the brain describes its search to describe.

In the swirling mnemonic thought dream there appears to be a center called a you, surrounded by a bunch of other things, some with a physical counterpart like rocks and trees and bodies, some purely imaginary like god and happiness and tomorrow.

When thingness is believed in by the brain that paints it there is the FEELING of being separate. As an imaginary separate part of this thought dream how ya gonna change the brain that has thought you?

You don't think
You are thunk
And that is unthinkable

No one is trapped in an idea or belief
That's a nice idea
Like you

She thought happiness was a thing and set out to get her some.

New year
New moon
New dawn
Won't bring the new you you long for
The one who has no desire.
The one who has only pleasant thoughts and emotions.
The one who no longer feels utterly alone.

Maybe you are desire and thought, maybe you are utterly alone?
Maybe there is no tomorrow?

Perhaps all you can know is this vibrant scintillating aliveness that
you feel. The symphony of perception and the simultaneous
recognition of it is the confirmation of this always on aliveness. This
flowing thought that seems to describe it seems to create a you and
experience, seems to create a wall between an inside and out. A
transparent window where there is no one looking out and nothing
to be seen until you appear, a reflection of a reflection of a
sourceless echo. A wisp of circulating memory that gives a feeling
of solidly. You know there is no solidity. You know this is it coyote,
and you know it is far more wondrous than you could ever capture.

The enormity of the un-captureable vastness of unknowing is far
greater than awe or love... the awe of awe, the amazement of
amazement, we are this flowing edgeless dreamscape that cannot
be swallowed as all songs sing it.

We crashed through the mirror
Every shard pierced our already bleeding hearts
Inside fell through outside and spit us out
Laughing and weeping drunk on love

The scent and sound of the memory of the rainstorm in last night's dream tastes like this.

The crest of the wave falling through itself
Wet in wet
Light in light
Where is the sorrow of no tomorrow that swallows itself in this overflowing brilliance?

How can a word capture this love? ...yet love and sorrow and joy and awe are words, as are we. The marvelousness of thingness when there are no things truly blows me away continuously.

Reflections of reflections of reflections, memory sings us into the song and our hearts burst as we hear our own majesty. Center-less infinitely faceted spinning jewels. We are a point of view, but it can be known and felt that there are no reference points whatsoever....

Most long to realize this is a dream
No one longs to realize that they are being dreamt

How long are you going to pretend that you are on a path to a state of perfection where there will be no more desire or anger or sorrow? How long are you going to pretend that all you have ever loved or will love will die and be forgotten?

How long can you pretend that maybe that overwhelming aloneness you feel may be true?

Many teachers of enlightenment tell you to rest as awareness or simply recognize awareness or clarity or open intelligence. This creates the idea that there is a thing called awareness, and perpetuates the illusion that there is a you separate and apart from what's going on who can do or not do anything or nothing to manipulate it.

Other teachers tell you to be in the now, creating the idea that there is a thing called a Now, and substantiates the painful belief that there is a you separate and outside of what's going on who can somehow join with this elusive idea called now. Can you find the beginning or end to a moment? Are there separate moments? Is there an edge or outside to what's going on and a you who can step outside of this flow and manipulate or accept or reject or surrender to it?

Some will say to stop trying to change or reject thought and emotion. This empowers the belief that there is a separate someone who thinks and or feels, and someone who does actions. Can you find the beginning or end to a thought or feeling? Are there really separate thoughts? You cannot find separate thoughts as you are not separate from the thought stream some call mind.

You cannot relax or surrender to what's going on, as trying to accept what's going on is what's going on.

Some say to let go of your story. This is impossible as trying to let go of it becomes your story, doesn't it?

There is no hope, is there? There is no other better more or next, have you ever found a next or now or then? Yer Fucked

This is it, coyote.

All that's going on, is an uninterrupted indivisible symphony of what we call perception and the simultaneous inseparable recognition of it. They are not separate and this edgeless flow is not an it. It has no edge or outside or inside.

The brain uses shared learned words to describe it, painting separate things, calling its own thought stream, 'mind', and believes it is a thing. Mind is not a thing, it is what's 'thing-ing'. You and all thingness arise in this indivisible thought stream. You are this flowing description. You are a mentally fabricated imaginary being.

Some imaginary 'things' refer to the physical manifested world which has no qualities or characteristics, or time dimension or measurement without this flowing description which seems to create solid and stable 'things'.

Other imaginary 'things' refer to things purely imaginary like self and god and tomorrow.

Many teachers will tell you that you are an unchanging thing like timeless awareness or pure consciousness or a true self or source or the love or emptiness from which all things arise. There is no thing which is unchanging as there would have to be things to have movement or non movement. There are no reference points whatsoever. There is nothing eternal as eternal is a long time and there is no time and there are no things.

This is it coyote, there is no other better more or next and no one to have it. All there is is this wondrous scintillating aware aliveness recognizing this awareness because of this conceptual reality that seems to appear through this dream of separation painted by learned shared words.

All enlightenment really is, is the profound shift in perspective when the brain no longer believes the conceptual reality it creates. It does not happen with effort or non effort and does not happen to the person. Yet it gives the imaginary character a life free from the ever present hope and fear and need of a never arising next, and free from the angst of knowing there is no meaning or purpose to life and that she will die.

Anyone who says that this can be taught or learned or given away is profoundly mistaken. They obviously believe that it is an understanding or belief or a thing that can be attained. It is an empty prize for no one.

This can be intuited and felt, this seamless edgeless ness of which I sing, but it cannot be touched with words. Therefore it cannot be 'known' in the conventional sense. You know it deeply somewhere, everyone does, this fluid un-capture-able unknowable spacious emptiness, yet because of the belief in separation it is rarely noticed.

The feeling that there is something horribly wrong is the dissonance between the belief of separation and the deep down feeling that there is no separation.

As long as you feel separate you will try to not feel separate, and all trying or trying to not try will perpetuate the painful illusion of and feeling of being separate.

There is no thing or non thing which you 'truly are', under or having thought.
No body no brain no thought no you.
The belief that there is something beyond thought is the belief in other better more and next. Beyond mind or thought there is no you. There is no beyond mind. As beyond is thought.

Looking for peace or love or enlightenment seems to creates a thing called enlightenment and a separate you, and an imaginary distance that cannot be crossed.

Self is the assumption of personal volition.
There are no things from which to choose and no one separate from what's going on who can choose. It's only marvelously thought which creates the illusion of separation. The conceptual virtual reality in which we exist.

We are the dream. There is no escape or outside to the dream as inside and outside like all this and that are made up. Nice ideas, like you.

How exceedingly beautiful to know that you and beauty are made up.

First crows
Punctuate the waves
Songs flow
Village sleeps

Morning yawns
Pouring honey on the sea

Hummingbirds don't even know they are. Without the objectified conceptual virtual reality created by thought there is no aware-ing of being aware. To know that we know. Amazed at amazement. Delighting in delight.
In awe of awe.
In love with love.
Life kissing itself through these lips this voice this song these very words words.
…Yet also there is no knowing of ideas like death...

He longed to have his teachers beautiful wooden bowl...
I cannot give this sublime emptiness away as there is none and no one to have it.

Brown leaf falls behind the shade
Caught in window's curtain
Spinning wildly

Love and death
Life's mad dance
Turns you inside out
Punctuates the syllables
That write your timeline
As you fall fall fall
Into wind

Scattered phrases dance on the edge of death
Waves of unknowing
Plow furrows of dreams
Unsown

Starlight beckons you
To take this footless path
These flames of love
Burn the caverns of language
Never heard
Never not said

Sunrise was yesterday's dream

Closer than your very breath
More intimate than your tongue in your mouth
Or your heartbeat
Closer than close this cannot be seen or touched

Noon day sun reaps shadows of midnight
Held in its own embrace

The taste of taste in circular motion
Spinning madly trying to look at the other side of the mirror you fall
through
Laughing and crying
There was nothing to get
And no one to get it.

It's not like you become one with everything, it's realized that there
never was a you nor everything nor nothing, no reference points
whatsoever.

The steps of his camel started to falter in the afternoon. He felt that
this next mirage might have water, and it did. Laying down under
the canopy of stars that night the fear he had held at bay for a
lifetime began to consume him. Maybe he would never find home?
He lost sight of his hands in the constellations as they swirled into
beautiful meaningless patterns. Strewn bits of light tossed by the
wind's reflection pulled him up into a vast edgeless flowing. A
darkness he had denied pierced his heart as it exploded into infinite
bits of empty.

In the morning the gypsies started to pack their caravan. He
watched their mirrored skirts reflect his weatherbeaten face and
realized no one had won the war with the stars. No one lost. A
sublime peace had filled and emptied him as he watched his
footsteps in the swirling sand.

Searching for a time beyond time
Beyond the ocean of death.
May leave you spinning
Until you recognize that this no time is all the time you have
This is it coyote.

Words cascade onto this page scattering waves of sorrow across
windows of transparency
Peering out into the unknown
Letters stretch across a leaking horizon
Invisible ink runs down my face

Sunrise waits until the crows announce the day. Waves have their
own rhythm, yet there is none. Caressed in my own softness, I am
the dream.

Such beauty when beauty is known to be made up. Such love
knowing love is made up. Rich and full beyond measure, this
unowned life. A center-less jewel, empty beyond empty yet full.
Measureless...

I am the longing to sing of what cannot be sung, and the sublime
melancholy of knowing there is no singer nor song without
imaginary others in the dream. The utter enormity of emptiness
overflowing.

I always am on the verge of tears
Not of sorrow or joy
Just the overwhelming wondrous ness of life as it seems to appear

We are the only being that knows the majesty of not knowing what
love is.

No Moon Empty Sky

Sun slides across sky
Sky slides across sky
Horizon unties itself
Sea falls up
Blue in blue in blue in blue
Ripples flow over and under into and through each other
Weaving transparent webs that catch the wind's reflection
Love's memories echo from nowhere
From everywhere
Not lost
Not found
Shoes dance on the terrace
Mirrored skirts swirl
Light cannot see its own face
No words can paint this edgeless emptiness
Vast beyond vastness
Empty beyond emptiness
Beyond a word
Like love
Like you

Scintillating spaciousness whirls and kisses you on the mouth
Where was that other half of a kiss I longed for
It was closer than my own lips
My own song
It was never mine
No one gave it
No one received it
It was never about me.

She roamed the empty streets
Lonely jazz clubs
Looking for the perfect note
Some soared through her heart

Others led her to the edge of the sea. In her darkness, tomorrow's day dream beckoned from the edge of no tomorrow.

She dove into the depths that washed the bones from her hair. She surfed into and drowned in her own reflection. She drifted into her own loneliness and collided into her empty shores.

I sat and watched my shadow burn.
Echoes of nothing sing this chorus.
Waves without a crest or furrow, this wetness streams through me as me and sings.

No moon empty sky.
No dawn will fill the vacancy in your chest. No words will the soothe the vastness of sorrow or erase your longing for freedom.

Carpet of day slides into view. How wondrous the morning glory covered with dew! How beautifully the wind caresses your softness! The love you were seeking created a path that had no end. Trying to erase your sorrow painted it across the sky. Trying to escape the walls builds them.

Cricket song recedes as night slips on its day time clothes. You find yourself dancing without fear of darkness or hope of light.

Waterfalls of memory slide into your crumbling footsteps that dance on the edge of time. Echoes boomerang across the cliffs and catapult words and phrases that cannot catch even a wisp of a shadow you spied dancing behind the mirror. You ran and ran as the edges began to collapse, yet the imaginary distance could not be crossed. You roared, and no one answered. You wept and found only a beautiful wetness.

Perhaps you are a beautiful reflection, with no solidity at all? All encompassing transparent brilliance has pierced your heart. You bleed into yourself.
The frame dissolves as the edges fall off the painting
Colors bleed into themselves

There is no ghost inside this body
Just a flowing watercolor dream painted by scintillating neurons
Nouns my bones
Verbs my flesh my feeling my dance of wet in wet
Space in space
Scattering syllables rippling memories and thoughts of future
A timeline
Braided ropes of air
Hangs suspended in sky
No ladder no bridge no compass no bridegroom no promise no
hope will lead to an imaginary destination of being real

It is very rare for the seeker to realize that he IS the seeking, the
looking for other better more next. Solidifying the illusion of
something solid to grasp and a solid separate grasper.

We share this beautiful humanness. It really comes down to that for
me. It seems after the shift that's all that is left.
Knowing we emerge and exist only as shimmering reflections of
each other is most wondrous. We have no imaginary existence
without others, and no actual existence at all.

Love needs no reasons,
Nor life

There are no words yet love is a word and we are words as they
pour through these tender lips, these sharp teeth, this aching heart
that we share in this song of life.

Trying to escape pain was even more painful. It became most
beautiful when I realized I only existed as a beautiful imaginary
thought dream, that self was desire, that I am this achy break-y
heart.
We turn around and embrace ourselves as we disappear into our
own desire. No longer is joy or sorrow or longing ours, no longer is
this magnificent life ours, we are this naked raw passion play of no
one of everyone. Truly we get to feel it all. Yet the road to this sweet

embrace was even more painful as we are this imaginary distance between here and here.

It cracks and buckles and burns in the heat of your own love and desire. You watch all the parameters of who you believed yourself to be collapse and your heart drops.

It's like you're looking for your own reflection on the other side of the mirror and the mirror explodes into a gazillion pieces and every shard pierces your heart as you fall through yourself.

There is an end to the falling when there is no one falling and it's realized there is no place to land, it's more like floating, suspended between love and nothing at all.

No safe spot, no place to hide, no one to run for cover, no better, no next, nothing other than this wondrous life just as it seems to appear.

Picking flowers
Ashes bloom in her mouth
The kiss of her own transparency

Velvet space
Thinner than light
This utter vacancy has no outside
Nor inside

No one left
No one followed
No one returned

Sunlight chandeliers fall through the tall dark forest. Illuminating a dead leaf spinning, a path strewn with memories and hope.
Birdsong echoes, waltzing with your breath your heart beat as you pause,
Suspended as the hush.

Thought paints a dreamscape of this and that. Colors slide into view. Sound shimmers on the wind. So wondrous how there seems to be someone singing these very words that slide through your thought stream that colors the world that you think of as yours.

Thought twists and twines weaving a bower of clouds where you can rest and feel safe. It may hold you for awhile, but for some the pretense becomes thin, and the cradle falls. You know there is no next, you know that there are no handholds in this slippery slide of life. You know that life is more marvelous than you could ever dream or wish for... what holds you back... what are you waiting for?

Wind carried her to the edge of no tomorrow and collided with the end of dreams. Sails collapsed under the weight of nothing. Rainbow iridescence slid down the canyon walls and gathered in pools of echoes. Under the shadows, not even darkness. Inside the inside, not even outside waited for nowhere. No one waited for no one. Ravishingly devastatingly wondrous this utter vacancy that swallowed the wind and roared.

Under her nakedness not even darkness, under this brilliance not even a reflection, beneath her song, not even emptiness. Infolding out-folding waves of sound unraveled tattered canvasses of light, her wingless feathers soared, love ripped wide open, raw naked and alive.

He drove all night looking for his echo and found himself on the threshold between forever and never
weeping.

Sun slid through its own reflection.
Behind the kitchen door
A moon Lilly blooms
Laughter at sea

There is nothing behind the looking glass
Looking

Nothing under these words
Writing
Nothing before or after this very song that sings itself
Echoes of echoes
Memories reverberate
Reflections of reflections paint thoughts of tomorrow
Nothing stays
There is no solidity
There are no things
Less than ephemeral, beyond all ideas of emptiness, the great
vacuum sucks out your breath your song your heart in utter
wonderment.

Empty stone
Empty sky
Empty heart
Drained of the blood of belief
Empty love
Feels like love eviscerated you
Ravished you
Emptied you
Emptied emptiness
And filled your empty shoes
Emptiness dances
Love dances
In you as you through you

This love song was never about you

The longing to share the knowing feeling of no thingness, this most
obvious sublime seamless ease, Knowing it cannot paints my
silhouette that dissolves into itself as it flows through this river of
song.
Trying to escape or manipulate the dream makes the imaginary
walls that feel as if they separate a you from the world seem solid.

The cage of words that you are can become transparent. However
all trying to erase your lines paints them and seems to shut out the
amazing brilliance that you are. That this is.
Right now just as you are. Simply and most wondrously this.

Life does itself
There are no separate parts
No one outside of it doing it
Or inside
There is no outside or inside
All imaginary separation
Like thought
And thinker
Feeling
And feeler
Action
And doer
Arise in the thought stream which paints the conceptual overlay the virtual reality of this and that.
There is no this and that without thought
Nor you
Nor mountains
Or clouds
Or sadness.

Or joy
Or love

The imagined 'problem' occurs when the brain believes it's own thought stream. It's horribly painful for some. They are called seekers.
Most try to change or stop thought to get rid of this painful illusion which, if it seems to work furthers this painful illusion of a separate doer.

As you are a product of the thought stream
How could you possibly change the brain that emits thought?
Yer Fucked

No thingness is impossible to understand. It is quite simply beyond belief. Yet it is always already the case. Once recognized, a hyper awareness of being aware takes center stage and there is a most marvelous sublime seamless ease and a simple joy and awe no matter what seems to appear.

Moonlit long shallow waves
sweep the sand
greet themselves
in and out
hello goodbye hello
Disappearing and reappearing
This kiss was never lost
It cannot be found
You hear it
You feel it
You are it

Empty of moonlight
Empty of shadow
Empty of wetness
Simply this edgeless sea of dreams
Caressing itself

Clouds race their shadows down the vacant streets
Full moon explodes inside her empty chest
She dissolves into the windy night
The treasure was the empty music box
Ballerina still dances
To the echo of sad sweet love songs
She is the memory as there is no one left to remember or forget
The primordial song of wind

no eyes apart from the seeing....
no ears apart from the hearing
no sound separate from the listening...
no wind separate from your cheek
no love separate from your heart
no inside
no outside
the horizon that held the sky apart from the sea
untied itself
the timeline from birth to death collapsed
as well as the time walker

she plucked the flower
to hold its beauty
wind
petals flying
loose ends of my hair

Dissolved as infinite kisses
Thousand petaled softness
Leagues of sky
Acres of dreams
Oceans of tears
Ripples of sunshine
Plough through deep dark sadness
Infused with interminable beauty
Simply full blooming aliveness
Bursting the seams of imaginary division

No one to be attached or un-attached
No one to feel sorrow or joy
No one to try to find the light
Or shut out the dark
Or dissolve into infinite beauty

I am moonlight
drifting pools of silent wonder
there is no source to this echo land
dreamscape
no center no edge no corner to hide in
songs have no place to linger
wind has no beginning nor end
yellow finch rests by the feeder
color disappears into night
this hush that has no answer
nor morning call
saturates the spinning
of light and dark

there never were any pieces of sky....
yet every shard pierced my heart

Roots reaching
Fingers reaching
Branches reaching
Hands reaching
Songs reaching
Hearts reaching
Rivers reaching
Life reaching to touch itself through you.

Never tied
With a ribbon or a song
This heart full of sky
Has no chambers
Or shell
Nautilus whirled and melted
Into its own swirling
Iridescence flows
Love sings

No one awakened
No one was asleep
There is no one dancing with love
There is only love dancing

Wind Paints Itself With Wind

poems sing me
I am this morning's song stretching my toes into the day
dawn reaches over the canyon and reveals light and shadow
dancing
colors the finches and sparrows
and their lyrical flight
robin bathing in the pond splashing
the rising curling dancing steam from my tea
disappearing

First robin song
Soft breath of morning
On my pillow
On the terrace
Long shadows fill
The space of empty moon

Colors burst open
The door of night
Mountains and valleys swoon
Cottonwoods in spring
Slow dance of wonder
Soaring down the canyon
Riding the winds

Light and wind
sea and surf
flowing through her as her...
Winged emptiness blooms

where is the beginning to this flowing poem?
is it a poem if it has no end?
what is this un-graspable love song that sings itself?

what is beauty if not this tremendous unknowing...
what is love
what is life
without death?

cloud castles forming and disappearing into a flowing stream of
wonder...

She watched her hands move methodically through the air no
longer searching for gems. They wove a cats cradle not intending to
catch anything. There were no things, simply arabesques of sky.
Bathing in the warmth and beauty of her own essential emptiness.
Hollowed out in between the lines
Pouring love

It is neither joy nor sorrow. It is a bittersweet glow that sweeps you
into the folds of itself and laughs and weeps with abandon. You are
it and it is you in the ever unfolding ever quivering tenuous tip of the
wave that seems to divide what has never been and what will never
be.
A sublime aloneness that can never be touched nor kissed with
words.

In the unknown deep silence lying in the very heart of unfathomable
depths. Love's blood lays at your doorstep and whispers are born.
There is a dawning of crystal blue waters flowing into midnight.
Falling into the depths of despair you become it. Reaching the
heights of sublime joy you are not separate from it, and soon the
quickening in your chest the heartbreak that broke you
fills you.

Reflections of moonbeams dance across the surface of my tea...
and I stir the starlight in and the miracle continues.... I dissolve into
the dream and laughter is heard echoing in the stars... I reached in
the moon and found the key to the universe...
Nothing need be said about the beauty... It fills you and draws you
in and you lost forever…

Songs slide into the vastness and I can hear the echo, it is me.
My very breath fills the sky with delight... I am filled with sky...
Empty sky spirals upwards and rainbows form and slide down
washing every pore of my being with love.
There is simply vastness appearing and dissolving everlastingly...
Starlight reflections in our eyes... seeing each other's multitudinous
sparkling... Dreaming an unfindable dance in the clouds…

All words are defined by other words
There is no one who understands what's going on
No one who is separate from what's going on who can capture it.
All that can happen is more description
Like this.

and description is not understanding.
Isn't it wondrous how all these shared learned words concepts
ideas paint the dream of objectified separation?
All words seem to bite off a piece of sky
Description seems to rearrange the sky into a place of rest or
understanding
But you know there are no pieces of sky.

I appear to exist as an imaginary character in a world of imaginary
separate things.
All perception and the inseparable recognition of it seems to occur
in this thing called mind, as in the night time dream there is also
light and color when my eyes are closed.
Yet I assume the physical world exists.
This body as real as rocks and trees.
This self as real as next.
The feeling of being a separate someone living in a world of
separate things disappears when the belief in separation falls away.

I seem to appear as a center of aware-ing inseparable from the
uninterrupted symphony of perception. I can only know what life is
like from this point of view,
Yet it can be known and felt that there are no actual separate
reference points whatsoever.

No feeling of separation from thought feeling sensation perception, from life.

Yet this is as real as it gets.
Somehow it feels realer than real.
This nakedness that no one wears, life full on.

This ravishing beauty of unknowing, of impermanence, of knowing this is it no matter what it looks or feels like brings utter ease. Knowing there is no outside to what's going on, no one who can step outside of life and manipulate or accept or reject or surrender to it. Nothing can be added
(Where would it come from?)
Nothing taken away
(Where would it go?)
This is it, coyote!
This precious aliveness that is obvious through whatever seems to appear.

Sea of warmth
Liquid silence
Is the wind free
Or bound by its own movement
Shimmering brilliant immediacy
Neither moving nor permanent
Is not contained
It's recognition is not a goal or attainment
It's always on yet
Simply uncatchable as there is nothing separate from it
Neither you nor me
Nor that cloud blossoming over the canyon edge
Needs to fill the sky with blue
Or paint the wetness in water
Words sing an imaginary cage
Around a day and a night
Around this tree and the Robin song
Around a piece of time
An hour a second...

Stitching all these words together
Will not sew all end everything
Into a seamless whole
This unicity has no edges
That have been joined
There never was a piece of sky for you to live in
No eternity
No now
Not even nothing separate from you

This emptiness you feel
Is the fullness dancing
In your heart you know
There are no things to grasp
And no one to catch the wind

Cold spring rain
Last plum blossoms
Sail down the street
Laughing
I warm my hands and belly
Steam from my tea
Curls and disappears
Night reflects itself
Dawn blooms
Diamonds on the window

Air swims through air...
Space falls through space
Light swoons through light
Tears drown in their own wetness
Life swallows me
As I drink deeply
Wind paints itself
With wind

The beauty pulls you in and you find it's you

Moonlight echoes softy
Beneath the waves
Rippling sands
Sing

Under the autumn leaves
Love wept
Waiting for a spring that never came

It never left
Your beautiful song
You never had to arrive

This dance has no end nor beginning without time
Time left it's calling card on the dunes
And ran away with the tides
That no one found or lost
In the dark
By the sea

I have no heartbeat without you my love
Here take my hand...

There are no words
Yet I sing
Every word a razor
That cannot catch what has no edges
Twisting sometimes into a vine that can break apart ideas of solidity
Like wind and water cleave the hardest rocks
Mountains crumble into the sea
Pavement cracks and you fall through
The ground that no one stood on
Love blooms and falls

Even plastic flowers fade...

Trying to catch the beauty
To wrap around and hide sorrow and despair
Your fingers turn to knives
Stabbing your own heart

There is no distance between you and here
Between here and there
Between you and your beautiful sadness and desire

These iridescent butterfly wings
Were never pinned
To this all encompassing light
This edgeless spaciousness
This joy of knowing this aliveness
Does not look or feel a certain way
Nor do you

Always beautiful
Whatever you think you are

I find myself in your diamond eyes
We exist only in this dance
The imaginary spaces between us
Twirling down the Grand Canyon of love

Two diaphanous wings flowing through each other seen only when
their ripples coincide

Nothing makes sense
And I love it
In a way that makes perfect sense

Still wind
Kisses my heart
I find no one kissed
No one kissing
And no one looking...
Ahhhhhhhhh
This sonorous lushness of seamless ease
This land, empty of even shadows
Is not the source of such brilliance

They are they separate
Neither are they one

Love wrote it's song in my heart the day I realized it was not mine
To find or lose
Or set loose upon the world

My pockets are empty
Of even emptiness
They cannot be filled
They were ripped inside out long ago
I am the tears of the many and the few
How wondrous to feel so deeply!
My face is etched with rivulets for our flowing wetness

Light dances and falls through a momentary shadow
Erasing the filagree where she had woven her memories of love
It was the echo of her footfalls that seemed to be heading
somewhere that collided with the end of tomorrow
Knowing now that it had always been this way
This beauty that flowed in around and through her was simply not
noticed

And where our hearts meet they flow into and through each other...
Rippling softly in this soft undulating love dance of this and that
Echoing down the canyon walls
Shimmering in the river
Wake-less rainbows reflect the faces of every one we have ever
loved

Pieces of sky painted with splashes of tears
Every petaled glance reveals
A mirror of what I cannot find
And no longer care to capture.

It is indeed like love
Illumined from within
From without
There are no sides when I look into your eyes
Your beautiful edgeless heart

Clouds dissolve and form and seem to catch the wind
Bareback we ride into the storm
Dancing freely
The scent of thunder
Fills us
Erases us as we
Fall into and through the whoosh

Sky and sea ricocheting
Refracting infinite shades of blue
She longed for the wet of wetness
The taste of taste
The love in love

She was a dream of love until she spied a reflection of herself
through a sideways glance in the storefront glass
Crashing through infinite shards of emptiness
She was left with only her reflection
Nothing on either side of the mirror
Her eyes only shone in reflected light

The magic she longed for...
was the longing

My world is not mine...
I cannot find any things to own
And no owner
Nothing solid or fixed
I can only find my feet when I'm dancing with another
Gazing into their beautiful beautiful eyes I catch a glimpse of my
own beauty
There is a wondrous ache
Joy sorrow love longing
Flowing along inseparable from the edgeless symphony of
perception.

There is nothing caught in this flowing
The net is simply words and concepts

This rich lush tapestry of perception weaving and unweaving itself, attention flows and rests, flows and rests. Only a tiny pinhole is ever noticed. Most is not noticed, especially the obvious non-fixed, impermanent, edgeless-ness of it.

Sometimes you hear your blood rushing through your ears. Sometimes you notice the yellow finches on the feeder, sometimes the steam from your tea, or the warmth sliding into your tummy. Sometimes the sound of the clock, ticking. Sometimes there is thought of yesterday or that time you last saw your mother. Sometimes there is thought of the coming day, or planning a trip to the mountains when the snow melts. Mostly you walk without noticing where your feet are placed. You may eat or drink without actually noticing. This all encompassing fluidity of perception is never separate from the aware-ing of it.

Thought seems to capture a part of this flowing, every word seems to throw a lasso around a bit of this edgeless symphony. Yet 'seems' is the key word.

Is any 'thing' ever caught, or do words seem to create 'things'?

Everyone knows deep down that this ever present symphony of perception and its inseparable recognition is all we can know. This ever blooming ever wilting, self creating self releasing momentary is obviously fluid and cannot be captured or indeed 'known' in the conventional sense. The 'known' world or the worded world is a conceptual virtual world of this and that. All description paints it, even these words you are reading now.

It's terrifying to consider that there really are no things, as you are one of these imaginary things. Yet if the essential emptiness of things and self is actually realized, and the blank isn't filled in with more concepts like true self or pure consciousness or timeless awareness, life is experienced as a seamless flow with no feeling of separation.

The conceptual world continues much as before, the stories continue to write themselves, although it is never again believed. Yet knowing you and I and love are made up, is not the end of love.

Trying to let go of
Or accept your story
Becomes your story
It's story
You are story
All the way down
Down is a story
Even story is story

It's simply amazing how shared learned words paint the story
All by itself
Just like this, the dream of objectified separation seems to appear!
If you look for what's looking... you may say
Well
It's me!
But it's just too scary to look to see if there's actually anything solid
or stable or fixed there
Or here
Or...

Fear of death
Plain and simple

You know deep down that life is precious because of its fluidity, and
you try to capture that magic
That precious aliveness you feel
You keep spinning in circles
Looking for your tale
Deepening the grooves of assumed knowing, and the appearance
of an imaginary center around which the rest of the world swirls

I stood on the banks of no tomorrow
Infinite reflections slid through my eyes
A mirror has no sides on this wake-less sea
Not even sound
Not even silence

A magnificent bird unfurled it's wings inside my heart and sailed
through its shadow

I never found it
Or lost it
The tides sing its unspeakable name
They called me back into the dream
It sounds like love
Like sorrow
Like nothing at all

Canyon winds
Strewn with sky
Brushed her path
With blues and purples

Liquid filagree
Star shadows
Painted her feet
No one walked
Or stood still
As this silence

No one wore
This sublime nakedness
Steeped in light
Subsumed with radiance
Saturated with this fire
That burns even its own brilliance

Simply this breath
This breeze
This thought
This feeling
This sensation
Without beginning or end
This all encompassing
Hush
Consumes itself

Just like this
Life has no edges
Cannot be caught or measured

Or owned
The hand that tries to grasp it
Is it

Awakening is the greatest emptiness
And the ultimate intimacy
Line less being
No one loses
Everything
And nothing
We were the lines that danced
Intertwining into patterns of love
We remain as these imaginary lines
That seem to create spaces in-between us
As we twirl down the Grand Canyon of love
Falling into and through each other

Echoes blossom and swirl
Wind paints plum blossom trails
Your footfalls need not follow
No path led us here
No one arrived
To this dance we have always been
This edgeless momentary
Has no location or time

Weaving and unweaving itself, life is lived in the heart of these
beautiful fringes where this and that are never separate yet dance
so effortlessly in the wind.
Oceans and sky and life flow through me as me, these words that I
cannot drink, yet paint me and swallow me, I am this empty poem
that has drowned in a river of song.

Tattered water color dreams swirl and no longer have any push or
pull on the moon or tides, or on these footfalls that no one takes.
They dance a love song where I find this breath that sings me,
sings you, sings a passion play of love and beauty and wonder.

Constant thought of remembered past and imagined future keep the dream of a person on a timeline between birth and death alive. When thought is no longer believed and separation is no longer felt, it's like time dies.

Yet here we are living and loving, with no hope and fear and need of a never arising next.

Seekers are trying to find the peace before or under thought, but this peace or silence is inseparable from thought and indeed all perception. It is the recognition that thought never actually divides what is going on. This deep silence is felt always, this knowing feeling of unicity, and as imaginary separation is created by thought, which includes you and mountains and moments, it's recognition can be frightening.

The seeker is like an imaginary piece of sky trying to glue all the pieces together. Every shard hurts. Yet there are no separate pieces of sky. Nothing the seeker can do or not do to arrive at this peace as it is either recognized or not. It need not nor can not be brought about anew.

Always simply this scintillating aliveness that you are, awareness aware of being aware, through this symphony of perception and its inseparable recognition. All encompassing, obvious, the big wow that you are has no edges. It is only in trying to grasp this magic, to arrive at what you are, that seems to push it away. Trying to gather the ripples in a pond is the rippling.

Whatever life looks or feels like, early morning bird song, words appearing on my screen, the softness of my cats fur, the refrigerator hum, thoughts of last night, of cooking breakfast, of calling an old friend, the warmth of my teacup in my hands, these words can never capture this infinite symphony of which my thought stream can only seem to lasso a bit of. Thought seems to isolate these bites of morning, to slice this into separate things and events.

Why cannot you see this seamless flow of which I sing and sing and sing, this inseparable unitary streaming? You know this deeply, this fluidity of life, that it is ungraspable, that there are no solid and fixed 'things', that there are no separate moments or events, but it is frightening.

There may be a longing as well to 'let go', but who would let go of what? Are there any things to let go of? Is there a you in charge of all this? A chooser of thought and feeling? Of what happens in this life? Did you choose your life, every thought feeling every perception? When did you decide to choose to choose? Can you choose to not feel like a chooser? Can you choose to not feel separate from what's going on?

Utterly spontaneously this symphony of perception and its inseparable recognition flows without anything needing to be done. Evenly and equally, it flows. Without any effort or non effort there is awareness aware of being aware.

That's all there is to it. All separation is made up. You know that. But if it's seen clearly that would mean that you don't get this. There is no one to win a prize.

Yet there is a sublime emptiness that subsumes the passion play that is no longer your life.

As beliefs begin to be seen through you feel lighter and lighter. You imagine that this feeling of freedom of lightness is the goal…. The end of belief in self can be realized somehow without the end of belief in thingness....

Both are unimaginable!

When they both go, it is the end of the belief and the feeling of separation. All thingness is realized and felt to be essentially empty.

Wow

Life feels like a seamless edgeless flowing. It is like a heavy load dropping to the ground, felt physically and psychologically. It never again feels like life or thought or feeling is happening to a someone or that a someone is doing life.
But that feeling of sublime emptiness is inseparable from the passion play that continues much as before.

Still there is weeping laughing loving, all infused with a most marvelous sense of awe.

Super Saturated with sublime ok-ness and awe
No matter what it looks and feels like
More amazing than I could have ever believed
This seamless ease
This sublime unknowing
This utter rest

Most seekers
Or all
Are looking for a way out of the thoughts and feelings they have learned are afflictive

They don't want to hear that we remain beautifully human
They imagine themselves in a future where they are unaffected by life
...Kinda like being dead

I am this nakedness no one wears
Yet most are trying to hide...

My flying carpet unraveled into sky
Tattered dreams of who I thought I was
And who I longed to be
Collided into the horizon between forever and never
As it no longer could separate sky and sea
Or you and me

No one fell into clouds of confusion
Or the sea of unknowing
Where empty bottles washed ashore
Containing no secret message
As the words had fallen apart
There was no one to know
Or not know
Or to look for her reflection
And fall into
fathomless depths

No one wandered along endless beaches
Between the vacuum of empty shadows
And the vastness where not even light
Or darkness lived

This devastating realization that there are no things, no self, no
other, no love... is ravishingly breathtakingly beautiful, and
heartbreakingly bittersweet. The unstoppable symphony, the
passion play, continues much as it did before, yet is never again
believed. Painted with sky in sky this all consuming brilliance is
never not noticed.

Still life dances and sings and does not move nor speak. It flows
and swings and dreams and falls in love. There is a wondrous heart
ache knowing that all thingness is illusion, that there is no one to
love and no you to love, that all you have ever loved and will love
are as real as tomorrow...

That this splendid uncatchable river of song has no one or thing in it
or outside of it to hold onto even one imaginary piece of sky. Such a
sublime melancholy knowing you are ultimately alone.... that this
imaginary dance of love, lover and beloved is made up of empty
resplendent costumes, of sideless mirrors, of a vacuum of dreams
where there is light and color, and music, but only in your eyes.

Still there is a magnificence of feeling deeply as there are no
boundaries in this nakedness. No signs or notes to follow, no place
to land, no dance floor to slide along to dance upon, to lie upon

when you die. Joy and sorrow and love and wonder have merged and become the backbeat of your existence. There is a wondrous heartache for all that seems to arise, yet never did and never will, for that sad lonely girl I never knew yet still see her spinning on the dance floor looking for the big wow.

Time shot an arrow into its heart and it was you.

you are your own perfect lover
held from the inside out in your own embrace
your own tenderness
your inside out heart

Cold spring rain
Drowns the morning
Ache of sunrise
Floods the dark

Where is the sunset
And the night that swallowed it
Where are the people
In last night's dream?

There is no here nor there to look
For nothing
For everything
No now nor then nor next
When it will be found
There are no lines around a moment
Nor lassos around a piece of sky
Nor a noose around your heart

The whirls and swirls in the kitchen tiles look like wings
Like turvey topsy love in a Chagall painting
Sun and light warm the day and sparkle on the waving long
summer grasses in my night time dream when my eyes are closed.
Just like this my world and I am painted.

Color and light and that crest of the hill

And the valley where I wandered
Painted day dreams, no more or less meaningful than the night
spectacle
Silent footfalls grieved the loss of tomorrow
As I was poured into this sublime line-less being
Transparent flowing brilliant liquidity
Sublime emptiness was revealed
When the vacuum of infinity
Collided with the dream of me and time

We are the paintbrush skimming echoes of reflections of liquidity in
endless waters... Colors shimmer into a beauty that only we can
see.
We can never see our own beauty. That is unutterably sad and
beautiful how we need each other to catch a glimpse of ourselves.

This desire paints my echo with sky in sky...
This longing to sing what has no words or melody yet contains all
words and all melodies...
tears
So beautiful these reflections of love's echo

Life becomes a flowing liquid love scape, a sensual cascade of
infinite jewelry flowing in you through you as you.

the incredible journey no one took
no one arrived
nothing was left
even the emptiness
fell out
Ancient arabesque of time
Extending infinitely without direction
Swirls around my footsteps
Moves through my shadow
Falls through my fingers
As if it never existed

Where was I going?
From where did I come?
Where is yesterday's shadow
As I wander here today?

Time bleeds through the cracks on the sidewalk
Creeps through the windows
Puddles on the kitchen floor
Footprints of blood
Going nowhere
Never marked a path
Nor caught a piece of today

If I am loves memories
What is my shadow?
If there is no next
Where will it go?

Time dances with itself
I could never find it
It was simply a magician's tale
As am I
A beautiful flowing story
In love with love

sound of rain hides behind dark windows
moon catches a glimpse of its reflection in the storm's sigh
morning is clothed in white clouds
what is revealed by this silence
that has never left

spring rains bend the daffodil stalks
dripping with tears
their blossoms gone

such a lustrous ache... the delicate tender sensuousness of life
streaming through you as you... love and love lost... sorrow, joy,
how wondrous we can feel so deeply...

...all of it a seamless embrace, a swoon of a caress from the inside
from the outside erasing all sides... the mirror was lost in its own
reflection and wept and wept at the beauty of its own tears...

without this and that what is there?
without the mirror of your eyes I cannot find myself
without these eyes, there is no beauty
nor love

nor mists swirling around the mountains
settling in the valleys
waiting for the mourning sun

We are empty echoes
flowing description
There is nothing underneath these words
No one having this thought
This feeling
This sensation
This life
A seamless flow without even a tear in-between the wet and the
river
The sound of no tomorrow sounds like this

A thousand winters cannot erase the death of summer

she would throw back her head and laugh
it was a brittle laugh
I wept at her beauty
one day she revealed her sublime sorrow
I wept at her beauty

she never came again to our bench by the sea
I see her singing and laughing and pretending
I weep at her beauty
the sigh of oceans
never crossed

I miss her and love her
they are not separate
nor are we

inside the mirror
there is not even emptiness

Always looking for the big wow
I could never find it
I was it
life found me and kissed my imaginary parameters into a love song
unlike no other...
Words simply petals falling swooning into their own softness
staves the lines that seem to contain the music
our imaginary lines bleed into a flowered curtain
that was never open or closed
it is all a play
light and shadow
and the scent of evening…

moon slides over the canyon walls
a bit of light still glows
drinking this precious flower
of this simple poem
where words melt into a flowing river
spilling onto this page
here is my heart
it was never mine

clouds only appear to clothe your nakedness
who could wear the sky?
who could wear the morning song
that sings you…

who could wear the dancing trees
or the wind
or the arabesque of light
that swoons into the canyon...
who could catch the sun
as it runs up the mountain into sky?

who could wear this love
this sorrow
this intimate aloneness
that has no clothes?
these tears
that no one weeps
never left the river
it rushes roars and silently flows down the canyon
echoes its song on the tall mountain walls
there is no source to this light this life
it drinks me
as I drink it
I am intoxicated

Spring reveals a leafless tree
Clothed in clouds
Reaching for sun it can never drink

Winds will never dance with these gnarled branches
Birds may nest in its hollow crookedness
The ones that need not hide

Nothing can steal this peace
No one can lose it
Or find it
Yet death may follow a river of ten thousand words
Sunk under its own weight
Of trying to catch the sunrise

No one sleeps under the tree
In the shadow of tomorrow
No one looks for autumn leaves
In summer

This brilliance has no source
Where no one drinks
Shadows dance with their own reflection
Wind sighs yet does not move
Without my tender cheek

I am the love the lover and the beloved
Yet I need you to dance, to find my feet
Come here, lets gather in the meadow
Where flowers grow on winters grave
All our dreams of summer
Gone
All our dreams
Is this dream

she was the ache of the evening
the song of the sidewalks
the lovers breath at midnight

moonlight flowed through her
as she was the light
and the flow
and the morning song that hid in tall dark shadows
sleeping

waiting for your lovers kiss
or your next breath
will leave you breathless

waiting for the words that will patch your broken heart
you will watch this love
this love
this love
you feared to lose
bleed into the world

an empty dress swirls
covered in mirrors
you are endless sky
and the morning glory
wilting

rain on rain on rain on rain
wet in wet in wet in wet
I am the rain song

and the hush
of no tomorrow

river swells
my heart bursts
empty songs
fill no silence

clouds do not hide the sky
nor rain these tears
nor darkness
this love

there are no steps to enlightenment
and no steps after
life cannot be traced
there is no past nor future

there is no one looking
no center or harbor to this edgeless sea
no wind that can be captured
no wave that is not ocean
no tears no sadness nor joy that is separate from you
enlightenment is not about not feeling deeply
oh my!
so beautiful, we get to feel it all!
it was never about your love
just love

the stillness of mind you seek
is the intimate knowing of this very immediacy
saturating the blooming of the flower
is its wilting
even though I live
my death is a most beautiful part of me

winter sings in the heart of summer

Forest Of Sky

Whose voice is it beckoning you to the edge of the sea? Is it yours, or the song of the ocean? Are there two voices or does this chorus come from inside and out? This is the love song you have never forgotten but you could never quite remember. Where is this deep deep longing? Why have you been standing on the shore waiting for your return when you have never left? There is no safe harbor anymore, there is no more pretending everything is all right. You have heard your name called and you cannot turn back.

Everywhere you turn there is nothing but vastness, and you realize it has always been this way. It was a beautiful dream that there were edges to the sea, and a sailing ship and clouds and sun and wind and direction and a destination and a tomorrow.

You cannot know the words or catch the song that sings you. You feel it's fluidity and I can see you swaying to its rhythmless rhythm. You are so stunningly beautiful dancing with the sea and the wind and the light as they flow through you. You have lost the longing to catch your reflection. There was never anyone who had an ache for freedom. There was no one to be free or bound. The knots untied themselves and revealed an edgeless wasteland where no one lived or loved, and you found yourself again, dancing between love and nothing at all.
Oh my! Here you are. Welcome home. I love you.

There is no way to sing of or convey this utterly obvious seamlessness. Yet I sing and sing and my words are tossed into the sea of knowing and may toss the seeker into that same sea.

I have never heard of enlightenment being a walk in the park
Yet the free glimpses are
After the ocean has called your name

You can never forget it
The longing to drown may outweigh the fear

Empty candy wrappers
Wind flowers on the beach
Dance with their shadows
Kiss their reflection in the wet sands

Dance is its movement
As wind
As mind
As life
A fluid dreamscape
Of light and shadow
Reaching out to taste itself
Through your lips your tongue your beautiful eyes

She wandered into the empty temple and found her hand print on
the wall.
Reaching out to touch herself she fell through the wall of no
tomorrow.

Sliding daydreams
Windows on the sea

No safe harbor
No one to land
No one to seek
No where to search
For that which does not exist

Mirrors broken
Shards of sky
Pierced their own reflection
Love bled into itself

Unclothed of nothing at all

She discovered she was this nakedness
That no one wore

No hangers
No closet
No room
She had no home
Not even emptiness
That no one lost or found
Only a shadow
Drifting across the threshold
Between love
And nothing at all

Sitting by the side of the road waiting for yourself to return... you
realize that you and all you have ever loved are beautiful thought
dreams sailing through each other, and it is sublimely bittersweet.

Love sailed away in her warm summer jacket.
Sea chewed her up and spit her out
She swallowed the stars.

Love is life is love intertwined
never not one or two
Or none
This all encompassing embrace
without edge or center
caresses fills empties
Ravishes
A vacant heart
That was filled with wishes
And became unbound
Un-owned
Un-known
Felt fully
This beautiful ache

These wondrous tears
These eyes that see their beautiful reflection
In this scintillating dance
Waves crashing, sliding on the beach
receding into their own wetness

A love without tomorrow
Has no words
Unheard
Unsung
The love in love

The taste of taste
On your lips your mouth your tongue

Light in light
Flows through you as you

Your eyes illuminate beauty
Love
And the sun itself

This kiss of one of two of many of none sears you beyond
recognition. Deeper than a lovers kiss or a broken heart, or the
knowing that no one remembers you as a child, that all you have
ever loved or will are ephemeral thought dreams like you.

There is no self.
There is no other.

This utter edgeless vastness without space or time or dimension or
emptiness sucks you inside out and outside in simultaneously, and
all that's left is the awe and joy of simply being.

Whirling as edgeless-ness
Looking for permanency
You cannot be caught
With spirals of ink under the skin

There is nothing under the tattoo
Blood and bones and muscles
And love are words

Wind sings
Through your eyes and the tree tops dancing
Like this
Love whispers your name

What you feared the most
Was your silent call to not be heard
Or answered
Here I am, sings the wind
Am I not your gentle caress
your tender breath?

The brain no longer believes the conceptual reality it paints.
Enlightenment is that simple.
It has nothing to do with you.
How in the world can an imaginary character in a movie change the
projector?

Life's ecstasy sings you as it's utter perfection. Streaming through
you as you is this very thought dream that paints reds and golds
and brilliant yellows and sunsets. Flowing cloud castles forming and
dissolving that no one ever lived in, and vast deserts and seas that
cannot hold a footprint or a tear.

The illusion of a world and a someone who is lonely, who longs for
a never arising tomorrow, who wishes upon a falling star to hear the
song of the universe, is the universe singing you.

You remember this song but you cannot find it. It is ancient it is ever
arising it is never heard, never not heard. It is a silence that shakes
the illusion apart and brings it together into a sonic boom of never
ending always ending never unsung awe.

Ocean falls into ocean
Wet in wet

Inside the inside
Light in light

Outside the outside
No sides
Space in space

He fell into his own reflection.
Empty of emptiness.
Slipped inside his own echo.
Deafening sound of no sound.
Falling through the falling
Dissolved of a need to land
No feet to fill these footprints
No echo will fill what has no edge.

No wet
No light
No space
Not even nothing
But this song
From everywhere
From nowhere
Fading as it emerges
A distant memory
A butterfly kiss

Never was a never
Or a forever
Or a now
In this current without edges there are no reflections
Simply liquidity.
All encompassing edgeless unowned love. It's simply flowing
reflections through the mind stream that you are.

Imaginary edges, mirror glimpses of being-ness reflecting in your beautiful beautiful eyes, singing these very words that seem to capture light.

Impossible to capture with the razor of thought
Yet I love this song
I am it

Fluidity of life has no edges
No beginning nor end
No observer can be found
Outside and inside emerge in thought.
Is the breeze separate from your skin?
Is this sweetness separate from your tongue?
Is red separate from the rose?

Words write the story of time and place and you and me. There is no outside to this conceptual reality thought paints, but you know that what's actually going on cannot be caught by thought. What if red were a thing you could hold? What if the wind could be caught? Where would you put it?

All stories are maps within the dream. There is no edge to fall off. All signs are pointers point back to the dream. There really is nothing solid and stable and fixed. No reference points whatsoever. Even the you that feels so solid, can you really find anything unchanging? Or is there simply a flow of memory thought sensation that seem to create a fleeting image, a flowing description of a person looking for an answer an understanding a place to rest and knowing deeply, perhaps fearing and hoping, that there is none, and no one to have it?

Fully alive fully human
Not looking for freedom knowing there is no one to be free
There is a boundless intimacy to life

You know life is precious and you want to hold on to it
If it could be grasped

You would have to be separate from it
Life in your pocket
A pinned butterfly
Has not the preciousness you seek.
You are the fleeting beauty of life
Kissing itself
Through your lips
Your song
Singing you

Who would want to grow a garden of cement flowers
even plastic flowers fade like old love songs... the beauty is in the
impermanency you fear and long for

Footsteps in the dark
Echoes on the sand
No waves can be lost or found
In this sea of dreams
The call of your loneliness
Comes back to you
The sound of the universe weeping
At its own beauty

First crows
First light
Soft breath of morning
Waves and waves and waves
A distant fishing boat heading out to sea.
This beauty this beauty this beauty
Life happening all by itself
Joy Sorrow Love
Loss of love
Life and death
We share this beautiful humanness
This ache of our aliveness.

Most spend their entire lives looking for more or better, in constant
hope and fear of a never arising next. Missing the obvious always
on beauty and magic and awe of simply being.

No other better more or next.
Simply this
Life streaming through you as you.
Through the marvelous imaginary conceptual reality of this and that
occurring in the human brain, there arises the most precious gem in
the universe. Awareness aware of being aware.

When imaginary separation is believed it is exceedingly painful
When not
Unspeakably marvelous
Words cannot capture this awe
Like love like bliss like joy

Silver light
Sliding water
No moon
No sun
No sky

Tears
Love's jewelry
Your only adornment

Prisms loosed their color on the glass
That broke
When you drank your reflection

In the dead of night
No hope
No fear
No time

Walking
Through memories of moon
A shadow resplendent in its own light

Summer sun dances
In pools of whispers
You know the words

You cannot echo
They fill your chest
As it explodes
Into the treasure
Of simply this

All the love you longed to feel yet you were terrified to lose
explodes and implodes in your chest. Your heart breaks so deeply
the very core of your being is severed. All that you thought you
were becomes a backward glance behind a mirror that has
shattered into infinite sparkles dancing on an edgeless sea. It is the
kiss of death, this love that eviscerates you, your lips your skin your
teeth your mouth your heart, your very breath is no longer yours.
Belonging to no one this love is everywhere and no where.
Streaming through you as you this seamless Kiss of Joy of sorrow
of nothing at all.

Your world collapsed
The curtain pulled back
There was nothing left
No one to wear the clothes of meaninglessness
Time fell through time
Slipped through timelessness
Sound reverberated in its own absence
Light reflected its own luminescence
Night spiraled into the echo of day
Beauty melted the edges between I am and we are.

This tornado of song that splits not even nothing into everything
remains. As you lightly step out into the edgeless-ness every
footfall blooms into an unknowable universe singing with an
unspeakable iridescence. You are this raw nakedness
feeling deeply
No one wears it
There are no secret pockets to hide in
No one left to hide

Life ignites itself as it flows through you

unafraid of love
Of life
Of death

Sea slammed you into sky
Sky into sea
In this utter vacancy between the horizon
Where there is no sorrow nor joy nor love
nor anyone to feel
nor anywhere
nor anywhen

Midnight heard it's echo in this ancient song
Of vast desert wastelands
Of waves of endless sand and ocean and sky…
This never remembered never forgotten all embracing kiss.

You have never left
Nor entered
There is no door or window or wall
This infinite spaciousness has
No ceiling
No floor
No path

No way

Running and laughing through the shallow waves
Sun smiles
A child picks up a shell

Your very own heartbeat
The song of the universe

It's all the dream
Even not believing in the dream
Is the dream

Step-less wonder
Cloud castles sailing through blue forming dissolving kissing the
sun. Constant disbelief, a most delicious unknowing, dancing in
footless shoes.
And loving love like crazy

Across the horizon
Birds awaken
What is the song of darkness
When no one is listening?

Midnight reveals
star-songs
What is the sound of wonder
When it has no name?

Footfalls in the dark
Echo in your empty heart
Love washed away in the tides
Of longing

It cannot be found
As it is everywhere
And no where
It kisses you full on the mouth
And breathes you

I spent many nights laying on a bed of nails
Gripped by unseen unknown terror
This is the part most teachers will never talk about
But I do

Enlightenment is not a walk in the park
Or an understanding reached by armchair discussions.
Or slipping into s state of bliss through constant mediation.

All your ideas about who you are and what the world is like or
supposed to
be are being ripped apart

As that is what you are
Ideas

It hurts like hell when you are beginning to realize that you are
nothing more than a flowing fluid thought dream.

It feels like dying
But it's realized you never had any actual existence at all.

It's the end of the belief and feeling of thingness.

There are no reference points whatsoever
And no one to grab one.

Walking through sky reflection
Sky slides through no sky
No contradiction
Not an empty song
Nor full

A child left his empty bucket on the beach
Was it very long ago
Time fell into itself
And sky swallowed you

I am not here
To paint a smile on the moon
Or fill your empty heart
I am a mirror
To show you love's devastatingly beautiful reflection and the utter
emptiness you long for and fear

We become the story of knowing we are a story

You feel alone
Because you are.

You feel disconnected
But are not separate from the feeling.

You long for highs
You are the longing
Life's longing
Only humans long for ideas like tomorrow or enlightenment...

The feeling of aliveness is apparent through all the symphony of
perception and its simultaneous recognition, whatever it looks or
feels like.
Self walks on a tight rope a timeline between birth and death, if
there is no one walking there could be no one to fall.

Drawer of dreams
Unopened curtains
Sunlight slides down your face
Cast shadows
Pool in your footfalls
Where echoes bloom

Stillness ripples across
the sounds of yesterday

Pirouetting into itself
Today sings
Melody and words
Burnt as they appear
Ashes of moonlight

Fleeting reflection of sky in sky
Nothing is held
Not even the clouds
Or beauty

Words are transparent slideshows
They cannot lasso a piece of sky
They cannot see themselves
Or their echo

Afterimages dance in a mirror
It melts into its own reflection
Knots untie themselves
Ropes dissolve
Yet the sky does not fall
Into an empty pocket
Of moon

On a distant shore
Beyond the horizon
Waiting for your self to return
Silence sings
Waves have erased your footsteps
And the stars

No dots to connect into familiar patterns
The path has collapsed
No safe harbor can be found
The very ground is moving
Like water
Time forgot to say goodbye

There is no retreat this time
This is not a glimpse
The war is over
This ocean of your tears
Your face
Is so stunningly beautiful
I can tell you I love you
But you will find nothing there
Just the wind
And sky
And an overwhelming vastness

No
The tears don't stop
They simply have no name now
They never did

You are the looking for certitude. For something called reality or peace or truth. But deep down you know that life is fluid and edgeless and there is no place to land, Nothing to hang on to in this hurricane. You may see your world of imagined truth and reality be blown away like a house in a storm. The roof the walls the linoleum gets ripped off the floors, even the concrete foundation crumbles, and the very ground it was built upon collapses. Like cloud castles in the wind, like sandcastles in the incoming tide. The very feet that seemed to wander the shores searching a safe harbor will be swallowed by their own footprints.

All ideas of this and that will be known to be made up, self a flowing mental description, a flowing thought dream painting the only world you can ever know, and you. A beautiful beautiful imaginary center of the dream around which the rest of the dream swirls.
This catastrophe is called enlightenment, and it is not a walk in the park. It's not an understanding as how could an edgeless center-less non thing be grasped with the razor of thought?

It's a toppling of the need to grasp what cannot be grasped. And a delicious awe and joy of life simply appearing as it does.

What is joy
What is sorrow
What is the hush in the garden
Moonlight reveals

Wrapped under winter's fallen footsteps
Lies an ache that has no name
No word is minuscule enough
Or big enough
To kiss her beauty

Love need not seek her shadow
Its in the ember of song that has burned in your heart ever since
you can remember
Without your eyes she cannot weep
Without your tongue she cannot sing
Without you
She is not

The thought stream is felt to be transparent. A paintbrush dipped in
iridescent translucence washes a surreal light show of people and
places and time
And love...

Flowing backward and forward into and through itself like the waves
on a shore less sea washing away the very tides that sailed the
moon into her shadow.

No borders are felt, yet I exist only as imaginary lines. Between
here and there, this and that, before and after, between the
between and through sides and sideless-ness, sublime seamless
ease pervades the dream.

Let us touch with our eyes so that I may weep at the beauty of
touching.
Let me feel the wonder of tears
On my face
On your face
On the faces of many
On the faces of a few.

The heart songs of the ancients flow through these lips your lips our
breath our hearts, it is only words that paint us and this primordial
dance of love of sorrow of nothing at all.

Do not the stars fall through you on to the path no one walked, or
are those your tears that paint this symphony of love? These tears
that have no name nor number saturate the earth. Your feet fall

through as the ground collapses and you soar as the wind. The music of love of sorrow of joy that lost its shadow and name as it flows through you as you.

You are the wind dancing and the soft caress of sunlight rippling through the trees. Without any place to land on this shoreless ocean the vastness explodes and implodes in your heart. All your secret pockets have been turned inside out and there is no place to hide, and no one left to run for cover in this all encompassing brilliance that has seared even the sun with its love.

Impossibly beautiful, this sadness that leaked into joy, these words that seem to sever the sky into clouds and mountains and deep deep canyons where the sun rarely sings, where only a breath of midnight ricochets it's echo into the symphony.

This music of echoes of light and shadow, of infinite notes that were never separate, this song that has no melody or time plays itself across my mind screen. A wind ballet delicately shimmering across edgeless seas, I am enchanted by the song that I am, that you are, that we are. The tears never cease, although you may not see them. Heartbreakingly beautiful this life, where we seem to touch, knowing we never really can.

Simply a wondrous thought dream painting itself and erasing itself like the light in last night's dream appearing in your skull. We hover in between what never happened and what never will. Thoughts of yesterday's love and sorrow, of winter songs and springtime flowers wilting on the dashboard in the hot summer sun. How wondrous thoughts of a never arising next stream through the backbeat combing the sands into an hourglass of time. Yet you cannot find your shadow in the desert dream without the reflected light from another desert dancer.

Here I am. I love you. You are beautiful.

No one lost herself
No one was found

No one lost her wings or her feathered feet that never touched the ground or sky.

There was not a someone nor a no one who left or entered the hall of dreams, where the walls are mirrors that resemble windows. They seem to shatter your reflection if you try to escape, yet may echo your heart song as you fall through yourself.

She was a passion play that poured itself into a glass of sky. A story book that lost its pages when there was no one to be free or bound.

She dances with the stars and wind and fire that burnt even her shadow as the wind scattered her reflection across the vastness until there was only the shimmering.

Yet she wanders the shadowlands and gazes at the beautiful dancers adrift on the sea of dreams. Love waltzes with love and she weeps at the astounding wondrousness of knowing she is dreamt that others are dreamt and only through their eyes does she seem to have any solidity at all. Dream windows open into an edgeless sea and the wind pours through her and she sings of the wet and salt and pounding waves that toss their heads back like a horses mane trampling even the slightest bit of ocean back into itself.

He spent several hours a day trying to let his thoughts flow naturally.
Never noticing that they flowed naturally the rest of the day...

I see you've bought a new instruction book on enlightenment.
Can't wait to get it home and start reading. Maybe underline a few parts. Maybe write out your favorite bits....

Doing that makes you feel safe doesn't it? Like you're going somewhere, getting something...
All the instructions you read there will only perpetuate the painful illusion of separation. They say do this, do that, don't do this, don't do that. It's even logical how this would empower the illusion of a doer isn't it? But you want to feel empowered. No one would want enlightenment, really. No one would choose to have all they

feel is true about them selves and their world and all ideas about truth and meaning and enlightenment shattered, including that there is someone to have a world. As you are those ideas, that illusion, how you gonna erase it?

I don't say that it's all a dream so pretend it's ok. I say all separation is a mental fabrication. All this and that and you and me and love are made up. Knowing that is not the end of love.

I am not trying to convince you as enlightenment is not a belief or understanding or philosophy or set of rules to live by. It's an earthquake a tsunami a catastrophe in which ALL you had believed to be true about yourself and the world including all ideas like truth and meaning and all ideas about what enlightenment is are ripped to shreds.
There is a profound shift in perspective that is felt physically and psychologically when it's realized that life does itself and has no separate parts or moments or time.

This shift is uncaused and does not happen to the person. It occurs in the brain.

And as you are an imaginary piece of sky lassoed by thought how could you possibly change the brain that thinks you?

This sun
This wind
These waves
This ocean
This shadow that slides down the path
Through the village
Through the morning
That stretches her arms around the cliffs
Pouring honey on the sea
Making shadows out of dreams
That walk
And dance
And sing
And weep

And feel the wind on their softness
That never dries the tears
That have no name
Nor shadow

Endless petals ever blooming ever wilting ever shimmering in the summer sun the midnight moon. The dearth of light itself casts a shadow in your heart when you are waiting to capture the beauty that you are.

A sigh a glance a cool wind from the north sings itself into your mind stream and writes its name on your lips.
My mouth my eyes my very fingertips are saturated with a love that writes its name in your reflection that I fell through whilst I was looking for love.

Endless echoes of love's reflection reverberate in this heart song that no one wrote yet that writes me.

A song an ancient melody where the words soar as infinite vastness itself weeps at the utter unknowable sublime spaciousness and the majesty of simply this... this life this life this unbound life that has no owner no home no place to hang your hat no bench by the sea where we sit as wonder itself and gaze at the beauty of each other's eyes.

I am flowing fleeting memory. Constantly forming and rearranging the liquid painting of myself. A crow feather softly sighs as it liltingly falls through the morning sun. The distant fishing boats heading out to sea. Song birds fill the cliffside and a squirrel chatters endlessly perched on the trunk of a palm tree. The symphony of perception and its inseparable recognition is far too vast to be captured and named, yet the wondrousness of the unknown and the worded world dancing through me as me... I am the wind and the wind dancing through me. Utterly transparent my echo flies across the cliffs and paints my silhouette with sky on a pirouette of wind that is unutterably beautiful.

Trying to run away from your ultimate aloneness...
Trying to fill in the terrifying vast emptiness and fear of unknowing...
Trying to find a reason for death and love ...
Trying to imagine a petaled path where there is no death...
Trying to figure out why
LIFE ISN'T FAIR!!!!
Trying to get back into the womb...
Trying to stop the trying...
End sorrow
End despair...
Find the treasure at the end of the rainbow...
God will fill in the blanks

Until the thunder...

Such an enchanting river of song... the music of love's heart magic
pulls you in. Beckons you to drown in your own sublime
melancholia. It's the ocean calling your name.

Love waltzed through my doorway and pulled the curtains as she
slammed me to the dance floor saying
Let's dance
It was the death of all ideas of love.

I never felt like I had a choice or was doing the deconstruction.
Never tried to fight it no matter how much it hurt... and it hurt like
hell. Far worse than I could have imagined I could hurt without
actually dying.

Even as kids we would sing sad songs about love lost and the loss
of youth and impending death and cry. The beauty of this
fleetingness was not missed. Playing the records again and again
lost in this sublime melancholia.

A self which is simply a flowing thought dream cannot manipulate or
allow thought or feeling to flow. Yet the brain which thinks can shift
so it no longer identifies with the under-mutter in which self and all

thingness seem to emerge. There is a palpable physical and psychological release when it's realized there are no actual things or non things and no one thinking, feeling, or doing life.

Many teachers say that they let thought and feeling flow naturally when thought and feeling always flow naturally. Trying to allow or manipulate thought or feeling perpetuate the painful illusion of separation. I would never say anything to empower this illusion. Yet this no thing ness cannot be grasped with words or the intellect as all words are the apparent razors that divide what has no edges nor center and what is not even a what.

The catch phrase I'm hearing these days is, 'I don't believe in enlightenment.' (Meanwhile the speaker of these words really wants it.) But quite simply they are right, enlightenment is beyond belief. It's not an understanding or a thing that can be taught or learned or given away.

Forest of sky
Echoes
Traces its fingertips
On your lips
Nothing was hidden
Under your reflection

Love another cloud castle
Dissolved in this mirrored glance
That weeps at its own brilliant transparency

Not even a kernel
Of someone left to know
Or wonder
Why

It is not necessary to believe in trucks to get run over by one
But there has to be belief in god to think he made it happen
Or belief in separate moments to feel that there was a single cause

All words are defined by other words. These shared learned words form the thought stream in which you and all thingness arises. No one has any actual existence, there is no one separate from what's going on to capture or know it. Most mistake this flowing description this roof brain chatter for understanding. But there are no things to put together into some kind of place of rest or understanding and no one to understand.

It's a never ending loop, looking for understanding, a place to rest, looking for meaning, looking for any idea like truth or peace or love or enlightenment. All that looking seems to substantiate the painful illusion of a seeker, and a solid stable goal to reach.

Most seekers and teachers believe that there is something solid and fixed and eternal that is not affected by thought or feeling.

How many ladders did I think I needed to touch the sky
When sky was all around me

Knowing you are a flowing thought dream does not stop it. It's like watching a movie knowing it is one and being in it at the same time. Laughing weeping feeling deeply... yet it never feels like the whole shaboogie is happening to someone or that someone is doing it. We exist only as these mental fabrications. There is no outside to this dream of separation, this virtual reality of this and that. All things are made up. Some imaginary things refer to the physical world like rocks and bodies
Some are purely imaginary like selves and next.

As there is no longer the filter of belief that there is a wrong or right way to feel or think or act or live or love or die, there is an intensity of life that's incredible.

A raw nakedness that no one wears... we are it...

I am a story written in time
Knowing there is none
Knowing I am a thought dream
Is my story
How is it that there is no one here and no one there, yet I drown in
your shadow and bathe in your light?
How is it that you will never read these words of this storybook that
fills and empties me, flows through me and forms me? I am this
heart song that pierced my reflection a long time ago, and left only
a two step of echoes ricocheting across the canyon. There is
weeping at this sublime empty vastness that overflows, a love
dream of footfalls at midnight gathering and separating, love and
love lost such a beautiful dance.

I see you, heart in your hand, terrified to lose all that love you long
to feel, as you read and practice how to be an unchanging rock that
is not effected by feeling. How afraid you are to feel the utter
sadness of your loved ones death, tears are your enemy, yet this
sublime wetness is the very substance of who I am.

It's gonna hurt until it doesn't
And that's when the tears start

I walk and fall in love all day
No one is a stranger
I passed a toddler yesterday and he looked up at me and smiled
The utter wonder I recognized
I wept all the way home

Trying to rearrange the sparkles in the sand to form a perfect
reflection
Of what, you never knew.

Looking for a song
You never forgot
Or heard

You are the longing to remember
What has never not been.
Nor will ever be.
Shadows float across the moon of desire
Can't you see your name
Casting shadows that midnight left
On your beautiful face
On your beautiful tears
Weeping for nothing
Weeping for everything.
The death of tomorrow
Shines

How deep the summer shadows that slide across the sidewalk to greet you? It is merely the tree tops laughing in the wind falling through sunlight to kiss your face. You cannot step outside the day or the feeling of wind on your cheek. You are inseparable from this wondrous ballet that leaves no handprint. It is fluid and has no edges as it seems to melt into itself. This ever blooming ever wilting immediacy cannot be caught and it's magic held, as you are not separate from it. There is no outside to this all encompassing day time dream where you can take refuge somewhere and manipulate the wind. Is there an inside and outside to a song or a rainbow or a kiss?

You cannot awaken from it as there has never been anyone sleeping. Your ideas of shelter and escape are simply the dream of objectified separation painting more and more lines that seem to define the illusion of a you who longs to flee. There is no outside to the dream as inside and outside are thought created. As you are a flowing mentally fabricated thought dream you can only know this worded world, this virtual conceptual reality, this magicians tale.

Trying to peer underneath the words
He discovered that underneath was a word
Trying to discover what was before thought
He found that before and after are thought

Sky surfs into its own reflection
Fringes of sunset melt in your eyes
Words echo into this dreamscape of memory and time

Words form and break a heart
inside an empty treasure chest
Where you waited
Late one night
You cast your reflection into the sky
But no answer was revealed
Only the wind dancing in the trees
Waving the long summer grasses
Rippling the waters
Sun dancing
So indescribably beautiful
You began to cry
And have never stopped

There was no wind
There was no soft cheek
There were no tears
That never dried
There never was a someone
Or a no one
To cry
Or listen to your tears

Most people stack all known things into a pile and call it 'oneness',
when there are no things, including oneness.
It's not that you and I are one, it's that there is no you nor me.
There is no one nor two nor many nor one.
No this nor that nor both nor neither.

We are flowing conceptual beings and can only know concepts, yet
there can be a shift in the brain that creates these bits or bites of
the symphony of perception when it somehow disassociates with its
own thought dream. This mentally fabricated worded world is the
only reality we can know, this virtual objectified reality is the only
place we exist.

We are flowing thought dreams, made of memories and thoughts of future...
How wondrous is it to know you are dreamt?

This feels truer than true when this hits you deeply

More intimate than your heartbeat or breath, deeper than thought or feeling
Deeper than deep... like a song you sang long ago but have never really heard yet it's always been playing...

capsizing all ideas of truth or meaning or anyone to have them...

You can't go back to the belief in separation
As you realize it was never really believed
There was no one to believe it.

There was never anyone under that beautiful rainbow dress of joy and sorrow swirling in the hot afternoon sun who was eviscerated by her own love.

No one wearing the clothes of desire who was ravished by her own desire...

Not even nothing was left in this conflagration
Yet there was not even nothing there to burn in its own pyre...

It's stunningly beautiful to know you are a flowing thought dream... that you have no actual existence at all
That you seem to appear only as reflections in another's eyes, knowing that they are imagined as well.

Someone says
You're beautiful
And there is simply nothing here
Vacant empty spaciousness
Yet in their eyes I see unfathomable beauty

Wandering the desert dream alone she slipped silently between the folds of nothing and collided with her own reflection. There was no path to nowhere as all signs led back into the dream. Finding there was no outside and no inside, there was a beautiful death of hope and fear and need of a never arising next.

We are the essence of life flowing
This slow sensuous dance without sides echoes down the Grand
Canyon of love.
These spaces these gaps these moments are imaginary
There is nothing which separates us
Only these imaginary faces
No one wears

I see your broken hearted beauty
Twirling down the canyon
Gazing at your reflection
Weeping
These tears are my persona
This laughter
This love

This banquet where no one feasts
Sumptuous
Life tastes itself
Sings itself
Through these lips this tongue this heart
That exploded and imploded into everywhere and no where
Such sublime edgeless beauty
That I am that we are
That this is

Carpet Of Moon

Shadows soar over carpet of moon
Wind scatters thought streams
Rippling into this sea of dreams
Sinking into unfathomable depths
Swallows the known world
Weaving and unraveling the edge of time

This sublime melancholia pirouettes into its own reflection and
mirrors your nakedness, it is this empty breath that sings you. Not
needing a doorway you dance on the threshold between what
never was nor will ever be. Light echoes from the stars and your
eyes and the welcome lamp that was never lit nor was never blown
out.

Love unfolds into itself, echoing a photoshopped copy of an old
rerun that dances to the tune of numberless voices and melts in its
own searing heat. Searching the map for a new horizon you find
everyone's deep untold stories aching for release. They gather here
before the morning breathes.
Like this, the same dance-step that no one ever took, flowering
and wilting between the hush and the day that sings you.

Infinite shades of not even nothing
Breathing, still, ...it seems
Yet breath a song that sings itself
Irreplaceable, this suspension of space in space
This flow of light in light
Where no ones feet have ever danced
And no ones lips have ever uttered a word
Or kissed the starlight in your eyes

Here, yet not
Come closer

I cannot find my tears without your beautiful beautiful eyes

You exist only as an imaginary persona
Not as a non self

And in the eyes of the few and in the eyes of the many, are the
eyes of the few and of the many.

How many decades did I try to peer beneath the words... I was the
belief that someone knew the answer to my unasked questions.
Realizing that no one knows more about things imaginary is a great
relief. Knowing that nothing can be known or grasped erases the
lines around an imaginary grasper.

I love watching the thought stream create all this flowing surging
painting color and light and shadow in the Grand Canyon of love.
And I Laugh and Weep at the majesty of life painting itself.

There never was a mountain she whispered...
Can't say here that it's ever become one again...

Same sun same moon
Same breath same heartache
Under this smile these tears these teeth this skin this mouth this
emptiness that so hungered for love
There was not even nakedness to be clothed

I am but a shadow of tears
streaming across illumined dust motes
Dancing in the stern
Of a ship that never sailed
No echoes lost or gained
Under my footfalls
In the hush
Of ancient songs

No longer looking for the treasure
Is the treasure.

The shipwreck of ancient songs pierced my heart. There was no one at the helm, no sails, no one catching the wind, and no one wearing this nakedness, no one wearing the crown. It tumbled into its own bejeweled iridescence splashing songs into its own wake where even love died.

Everyone including myself seem like echoes of people I once knew. The river leaves no fingerprints on its own sublime wetness, sad and beautiful these tears that are my very substance.

Ok
Here's what it's like:
You've heard of the third eye opening, yes?
When this shift happens it's like there is a realization that it was never shut. The physical eyes continue to see in binocular vision, yet the third unseen intuited eye knows and feels that there is no division. This feeling of edgeless seamlessness permeates the dream of objectified separation.

Combing the clouds for teardrops she found only empty sky
She tried to pour the ocean into a paper cup so she could taste the vastness
Folding it into an origami heart
It sailed into itself
Leaving only a wake-less wake of unspeakable beauty
The wind left the sails that now caught her reflection
Merging with the colors of sunset
Memories of smiles and tears dissolved into the trackless ocean
That no one crossed
This salty sweetness that
No one swallowed

This ravishingly stunning emptiness
That no one
No thing
filled

It seems that spiritual is the feeling that there is something more
better other than this what seems to appear.
As enlightenment is knowing there is not, it has nothing to do with
spirituality

If I call your name do you not answer?
I am as real as you. As real as tomorrow as real as yesterday. We
exist only as these imaginary characters. It isn't oneness or
emptiness pretending to be someone. It is all pretense and there is
no one or thing pretending. There is no other better more or next.
This dream of objectified separation is the only place we exist. This
is it coyote, your one and only life except it's not yours.

This precious immediacy is all we can know. Rich and lush, vast
beyond measure, we can not know it in the conventional sense as
it is edgeless, all encompassing, and has no outside to it where we
can go to capture it or accept or allow it or reject or manipulate it
or add something to it or take something away. There is no outside
or inside, as all qualities and characteristics, all time all
measurement, the worded world of this and that is created by the
thought stream.

There is no other better more or next yet thoughts of these,
thoughts of past, are included, in this uninterrupted indivisible
symphony of perception and the simultaneous inseparable
recognition of it. Neither awareness nor perception are things, nor
are they one big thing. All 'thingness' is seemingly created by
shared learned words and concepts. This imaginary thingness

paints the known virtual conceptual world, the dream of objectified separation.

This conceptual world is the only world where we exist. This virtual reality is the only reality we can know, yet it can be intuitively known and felt that all separation, all thingness, this world of you and me and mountains and valleys is made up. A mentally fabricated wondrous world where love and beauty and wonder exist.

Deep down this is felt, that there is no solidity, that life is fluid and edgeless, but this can be very scary. What if you have no permanency, what if there is no permanency, what if nothing can be known, what if there is no other, no better, no next?

This intuited knowing of edgeless-ness creates a dissonance with the belief in thingness, the belief in solidity, the belief in next. Belief is thought that seems and feels real and solid. This dissonance hurts. For some it is exceedingly painful and they are usually the ones who become seekers. Looking for truth and meaning... not realizing that truth and meaning are yet more concepts like them. Often they try to escape not realizing that their imaginary lines are fortified by this effort.

There are no edges to what is going on, are there? Can you find an outside to what is going on? Can you find the beginning and end to a thought or feeling or moment? Are there separate thoughts feelings or moments? If you cannot capture them it is because you are not separate from this stream of perception and it's recognition.

This magnificent ever emerging ever dissolving momentary happens quite spontaneously all by itself. There is no one or thing making it happen. It does not happen as it's supposed to or as its meant to happen. It simply happens. It is neither right or wrong, yet feeling that it is wrong or right may occur.

All perception arises equally and evenly without anything needing to be done, and it is simultaneously recognized without any effort or non effort. The feeling of effort and the feeling of ease both arise effortlessly.

There is nothing the seeker can or cannot do to recognize that this is it, that they and all thingness is made up. As all trying or trying to not try perpetuates the painful illusion of separation, of a try-er, of an imaginary next when this will happen. There is no next and no one to get this or arrive at this imaginary special place of enlightenment.

This profound shift in perspective can occur but it is not an understanding or belief or a slipping into a state of constant meditation of bliss or peace. There must be a ripping apart of all ideas of what you believe to be true about yourself and the world including all ideas of truth and meaning and that there is anyone to have a world. As you are those beliefs how can you erase them?

This is truly an empty prize for no one.

No one knows what's going on. All we can know is ideas concepts descriptions of what's going on that seem to capture part of it, and are a part of it. All description seems to create solid stable things, like lassoing the wind or throwing a net into a river, or pining a butterfly to a board, they cannot capture this wondrous fluid aliveness that is so obvious.

Even calling it unknowable or a mystery seems to tag it and make it into a thing. Most mistake description for understanding.

The knowing feeling that what is going on IS unknowable and ungraspable and fluid can leave most scrambling up the banks with their net of words trying again and again to stop that feeling of falling.

Knowing without a doubt that you are not separate from this flow of thought feeling and perception there is no longer any hope or fear or need of a never arising next. Knowing that this is indeed it, there is no attempt to escape the only world you can know. There is utter rest and a sublime ok-ness with whatever seems to appear.

What you had feared becomes most wondrous.

The precious gem of impermanence, of unknowing is the beauty of life itself.

Emptiness so vast it has no vastness rushes in and plunges it's heart into yours and it's a perfect fit. Bereft of purpose or time the dagger that pierced love itself eviscerates you and scatters your shadow in the wind. You had no solidity at all, you were simply memories that left no footprints, that had no pull nor push nor tides that sang a sea shanty of joy and sorrow, and of vast edgeless moonscapes that drifted across an empty silhouette. Etched with sky in sky no lines could could be traced, yet you discovered your reflection weeping at the enormity of this unknowing, at the magnificence of this timeless dreamscape where no one was lost and no one was found.

This vastness pulls you right back out of the bottomless depths where your echo fell into the sea and drowned in the fiery promenade of the setting sun. The oceans sing your nameless name with the tides that lost their momentum as they slammed into the rocks below the weight of this darkness that pours into itself through your heart. There were no hands to hold it, to measure its lonesome tracks in the sands that were always falling through an hourglass that lost its reflection when you fell through.

This rich unnamable vastness of utter unknowing sings a symphony of light that dances through its own light. It has no name, not even beauty nor love, yet everyone knows it. It is always on the tip of your tongue and yet the words evade even the most fluid poetry. It cannot be sung nor heard, but it's in the wind caressing your softness and the tree tops dancing, the long grasses waving hello goodbye hello. It is obvious always this magnificent aliveness that sings itself and has no need to borrow words to pinpoint itself on a map where there are no paths nor signs as everywhere and no where is always here. There is no there and no one to leave or arrive, you have always known this, this embrace of life that has no beginning nor end yet is always blooming and wilting. Without time or measure the blossoms are the color in your smile and the wetness of your tears.

What you feared is true, you are simply a flowing lovers kiss of thought feeling and sensation. You have no solidity at all, but you never did, so you cannot stop the falling into the falling that has always been on since the day you learned your name and that you will die. There are no handholds no places to land and there is no one to land, only the whoosh falling through the whoosh. Light falls into light, space falls through space and yet you turn when I call your name.

There is no one to be a no one or a someone, you are pretense yet no one is pretending. You are utterly naked yet there is no one underneath your nakedness, no one wearing a smile, no one weeping.

footsteps in the dark
footsteps in the light
morning sings

nothing was left
nothing was gained
not even sorrow
or delight in the wind

playing in sunlight
beauty bathes melancholy
bathes joy
bathes your empty footfalls
as they crumble

bathes your appearance
and disappearance
child like wonder
recognizes itself

reflections dance across the canyon of empty shadows

pools of echoes
shimmer
singing day and night
and infinite colors

piercing me as it sings me
this wonder
my very breath
my very heartbeat
my very song
is not mine
nor yours

is it ours
we walk nakedly
together we find our hands
our hearts
our breath
our song
this love
this life
this unknowable
fleeting
magnificent
aliveness

What is sorrow
What is joy
What is the sound of a plum blossom
Falling

What is the distance between the death of tomorrow?
Why is the song of midnight so beautiful?

Infinite hues of shadow echo and soar
Surge and subside simultaneously

Paint the night time streets with footsteps
Plum blossoms swirl around my feet and
Dress the winds of memory

Nothing was caught or lost
No one wore this dress
This web of sorrow and joy is empty yet
Shimmers in the streetlights
As it self releases
The taste of my own lips
Fills a paper cup of moon

Drinking deeply
Life swallows itself

Awareness is not a thing, perception is not a thing. There are no things nor non things, not even one really big thing. No selves or bodies nor anyone or thing to know this. There is no true self that is programmed or learns ideas. There is no one or thing that has beliefs or thoughts or feelings, no one who is hypnotized, no one who is asleep and no one who awakens.

There is only this dream of separation, this virtual conceptual reality that no one has written or created, which can include the knowing that the self and all things are made up. That this is indeed a virtual reality is part of the movie. All description of this is it, including this.

There can be a knowing that this, just as it seems to appear is it, that there is no other better more or next. There is a seamless ease that permeates the movie when separation is not believed or felt. This all encompassing edgeless wholeness is recognized to be the story, this recognition that there is no outside to the fiction destroys all hope and fear and need of next.

There arises an ever present awe knowing that there are no things nor non things yet things and selves seem to appear. The awe at this obvious unexplainable aliveness that arises all by itself, looking and feeling like anything at all.

You may reach a point where you have read all you can read, where every hand you've held starts to dissolve and every bright promise of a future starts to fade. You begin to fall into this sinking feeling that there's nothing else than this… ever gasping for breath you turn around thinking maybe you could go back to another time when you believed all the lies but there's nothing there you can't even find your shadow or your footsteps

I used to read entire books to have a brief moment of feeling like my hands were off the handlebars. I found some texts that seemed to leave my mind hanging again and again. Some people tell me that they have copied me reading my poems onto their phones and listen while driving. They say it's soothing.

Do I want to soothe?

Perhaps it is a becoming accustomed to not knowing. Getting used to the indivisibility which is always on.

Death gives life its sparkle. Concrete cracks and wood weathers and rots and flowers wilt, even plastic flowers fade. The ever blooming ever wilting edgeless momentary is all we can know and we are not separate from it.
There is no source nor anyone dancing.
This is a center-less side less seamless all encompassing dance. Without beginning or ending yet always beginning and always ending. There are no things to be grasped and no one grasping.

This fluidity this impermanence may be frightening. Yet you know deep down that this is so. This has been following you around like a hungry dog since the day you learned to write your name, the day you learned that you would die. You cannot turn around and face it as you are it. it is truly your own love that will ravish you and eviscerate all ideas of permanence and certitude.

Beliefs are like life in a strongbox. No light can enter when they've painted the window of unknowing shut.

How long are you going to pretend that you will never die?
How long are you going to pretend that there is a God or
consciousness or some loving force looking out for you?
How long are you going to pretend that you are on a road to a
place of perfect love and peace and bliss where no one is angry
and everyone loves each other forever?

There is no place to rest, there are no handholds, you are falling
and have been since the day you were born. When the whoosh
falls into and through the whoosh, when never and forever collide,
when you realize that this is it, just as it seems to appear, you
realize that there is no other better more or next. That there are no
separate things or moments to be perfect or non-perfect.

Your heart drops and all that love that you were terrified to feel for
fear that you might lose it floods your being. This knowing feeling
that you are not separate from life what ever it looks or feels like,
there is a simple joy and ease and quiescence that is undeniably
the peace the love you have always sought and you know that it
has always been this way. You just never noticed.

Shadows swirl from the tree tops
Spilling onto these pages
Saturating these words
That bleed onto the sidewalk
Pooling in echoes of their own reflection.

Love sings it's bittersweet song
In waves of sorrow and joy
The loss of tomorrow
Catapulted you over the rainbow
Until all was treasure
Your beautiful shining tenderness

Whose words were pressed between the pages of your heart
Not yours or mine
When the binding of belief unraveled
Autumn leaves soaring
Clear blue sky
Self illumined wonder

I can hear you singing softly
In the morning birdsong
In the afternoon winds that caress my face
In the colors of the end of day
That no one won
In the midnight hush
That led nowhere

and her words flowed like liquid sunshine pouring through an
empty prism and melting the coldest of hearts...........
...and when the sigh of un-knowing un-trampled the grasses where
love lay bleeding......
the sun rose on her nakedness and a wind of perfection kissed her
cheek where tears would never dry

Hope and fear
The guard dogs of the heart
Rip you to shreds as you fall through
The mirror of who you were crashes into its own reflection.
Leaves no one standing
Blood pools in concert with its own redness
Astounded at the fluidity
That has no direction
Wet in wet in wet in wet
This and that dancing
Splashing in waves of pure iridescence.

Edges within edgeless-ness
Form within formlessness
Color and light illuminating a shadow that no one wore...
No ones hands were lost or found
Yet they seem to play the game
Casting shadows
Skipping stones
Across the ripple-less sea

Ancient patterns in a threadbare carpet
Echo and hum yet cannot be traced
Sunlight shifts across the fibers
Attention moves and rests
Inside and outside have merged
Plum blossoms pirouette down the street
Wind breathes me
Silence of unknowing
Sings throughout the day
A gentle wonder
Dances

Weaving echoes as they sing themselves and untie the sky, sky un-
ravels blue from blue from blue from blue...

It is only in this dance that leaves no footprints where words can
soar through the shallows and dive into unfathomable depths.
They swallow the sun and submerge your heart in wetness that
leaves a landscape of tattered rainbows. Scattered treasure flows
into itself and recognizes its own magic.

The timbre of life, the sweetness of sweet is this very aliveness...
so utterly obvious but missed when imaginary separation is
believed in.

Yet when were you ever separate from perception? From a tear
sliding down your tender cheek or the feeling of the warm summer
wind that dries it?

In the shade, in the shadows, love lies nestled underneath the
fallen leaves.
In the garden midnight dances and you follow your footsteps into
the fecundity of life.
Such brilliance cannot be missed
Or kissed
Light falls through light and explodes into this very love song.

This heart has never been contained in a treasure chest.
Feeling exceedingly deeply I never wanted to not feel so much, it
seemed like others had callouses I did not.
Yet knowing there are no others.... feeling their intense beauty...
whispering I love you constantly under my breath under these
words soothes some lonely aching hearts.

Now there is no concern as to whose pain whose sorrow whose
joy... whose words, whose footsteps were dancing late last night
wrapped in the broken hearts of everyone of no one, caressed by
the last breath of the song of midnight.

Echoes Have No Source

Sky flowers bloom and fall
Mountain appears through the mist
Empty footfalls end
Echoes have no source
No one was going anywhere
No one was going nowhere
No one arrived
No one was left behind
No one disappeared

There is breathing
Weeping
Laughing
Toasting the sunset
Colors swirl in my glass
reflecting ideas of emptiness and fullness
Dancing

Drinking deeply life
Life drinking me

Tsunami of love soft and fierce, caressed and split apart my heart.
Like tender delicate rootlets growing deep deep deep breaking
heavy boulders, tentacles of utter emptiness untied the strings that
held up the sky and surging waves exploded into infinite wetness.

Were these my tears that reigned iridescent jewels into rippling
meadow streams into deep canyon rivers into edgeless seas where
I once set out on a wooden boat looking for my dreams and
discovered that I was the dream...

Wonder strolls through the morning
Showering golden leaves across this path
Tracing these steps in echoing sky

And who walks
And who marvels
And who weeps endlessly of this unfathomable life that sweeps
sorrow and joy into piles of autumn leaves that scatter again in the
evening wind

The planting of the flower bulbs was enough
...he did not need the spring

Echoes reflect scattered footfalls
Tree tops dance in the wind
Golden leaves soar down the canyon
The hush before sunset
sings

Wind rustles ideas of emptiness into songs
soaring freely through this mind stream
Painting blue on sky

caress of wind
my breath
ideas of inside and outside scatter
mountains appear through mourning mist

Pieces of sky shimmer dance, and rearrange themselves into
castles in mid air. You look down and find your feet have never
been on the ground, and they begin to look as empty as the
vastness, and it is, you are, like a moving all encompassing
bejeweled three D light show, indeed it is wondrous beyond
measure this dream that you are.

Your boat always had a leak, you were the shimmering on the
bottomless sea.
Falling happens, wings grow silently, screaming.

Iridescence flows seamlessly with light, bottomless oceans, deep green-y blues, untold mysteries are born rising to greet the sky and drowning in their own loveliness, never captured, now unsought, seamlessly dancing in between a breath and nothing. They blossom into themselves and delight in their own beauty, and petals fall and kiss their own reflection. One brief shining brush of winged breath, and the hush of nevermore.

We are the moon and stars and the light shimmering in imaginary spaces as we fall into our own reflection, our own beauty, shining. That which you longed for, trying to catch the rippling water in your cupped hands, you saw your own face as your tears kissed themselves. You fell through your own echo, no longer trying to capture the sweetness, no longer looking for solidity there is no fear of falling, of life of love, of death. Such unimaginable beauty, this fragility this tenderness this tenuousness this wetness, the shining of our I's. Trying to catch the beauty seemed to create an imaginary distance between us and it. There was never any separation.

Cottonwoods in the canyon waltz as I breathe. The heaviness the lightness the weight the fullness the richness the intoxicating dance with no edges or center. The dance floor has fallen away and I cannot find myself.

I am the dancer and the dance. I am the golden leaves swirling flying falling shimmering in the long sunset light. I am my breath and the song and the wind flowing through me as me. There is no doubt and no place for it to arise that this is who I am,
this is who you are.

Clouds no longer seemed to block the light and warmth.   Wings were no longer needed to soar. Basking in ever present uncontrived ease. Dancing on the boardwalk and falling through the cracks. Waves crashing at your feet. Bathed in sunset fire.

Without her costume, she could not dance. She knew without it she did not exist. No one wore her nakedness. She found herself only in the touching.

Words flow in around and through the emptiness and never touch it,
yet they create castles in mid air, where we live and love.

words seem to capture space in a box
a brick
of nothing
meaningless
yet appearing to mean something

a wall an edifice

a blanket a shield
a barrier

light
aches to get through

your heart
aching
to be ruptured
to be broken

forever

Writing backwards across the sky
Tears up your reflection
Rips away your footfalls and their echo

Jewels gleam untouched
Ungraspable facets cut through their own sparkling

Like a knife in the soft palate of your heart

Tasting the fullness
You dream of more…
and you are lost forever in your desire to know to capture to hold
the un-holdable

Until the spark the ember the fire of your own love burns your hand burns your heart to the ground and your ashes are swept away by the winds of your own desire

Love's memories paint this nothingness into a flowing dreamscape of you
spaceless being-ness
like a reflection on a ripple
an echo in a dream
there's nothing to find and no one to find it

and life is neither lost nor found when it's no longer yours

it is sublimely serene

ahhhhhhhh... the sound of rain on the fabric of my umbrella. Streetlights shining through, this golden light painting a jeweled surface on the black nighttime pavement. Drops like precious gems sparkle against the dark sky, and the radiance the brilliant shining transparency of this empty luminosity, this naked fleeting momentary...

And love flows. That is its nature, it flows like water eroding and erasing the imaginary edges that define things, and it is unmistakably the precious gem in this ungraspable sparkling stream we call life.

Surfing down an endless rainbow, infinite hues flow and surge. Effortlessly you merge with sea and sky and light and space, as you have never been separate. The water cascade dance subsumes you and floods every hidden corner of your being with the most wondrous sense of completeness and utter okay ness and magnificent awe. Vibrantly alive the fullness bursts into endless vastness. Never caught or contained the wave drenches the sea with its own wetness and is subsumed in your bottomless depths.

How you longed to capture this surge of life...
Chasing your tale created a spinning that seemed to have a
center...
Forever trying to grasp space felt like a caress of air between your
fingers, and a tingling notion deep inside that your hands would
forever remain empty.

how can one recognize the futility of trying to grasp life trying to
hold it
trying to stop it
right here right here right here.

as if you could swallow the sky
and paint the blueness in your heart forever.
but what is blue
what is sky

what is that ache in your heart you have felt your entire life?

and you rush around looking for that missing piece and the spinning
seems to have a center that when sought is obviously empty.
and the breezes created by your spinning skirts carried their colors
into the sky
red and blue and yellows unfold
a kaleidoscope of perfect wonder tossed itself into the evening
breezes falling flowing gently down the canyon.

a caress you had always longed for was always here
it was your own fingers tingling on your skin
Traipsing over your body
rainbows sobbing at the color that could not be found
or lost

there were no steps needed to find what could not be found
yet a dance most sublime
as the cottonwoods waltzing
golden leaves falling
gently into waves of color brushing your footless steps

Every word seems to cut up what's going on into separate bits, including a separate you. It is exceedingly painful if separation is believed. It feels like the sky has come crashing down and broken into infinite shards of blue, and theres a definite feeling of not all rightness, like a hole in your heart that is being stabbed constantly, and theres a desperate anxiety always on, like time is running out.

That big internal clock that drives you to try to put the pieces back together, and the sharp edges hurt. When it feels hopeless we grab for any 'glue' we can to try to patch the sky. Usually more learned ideas of what the sky should look like. Desperately trying to find some meaning, some safe harbor, as we are drowning in our own tears.

and somehow.... no one knows how or why, it's suddenly seen that there were no pieces. As we have many many cuts and ripped apart skin heart blood bones, all these shredded ideas like worn out bloody bandages fly away in the wind.

Blue in blue in blue in blue
There were never any separate pieces of sky yet these shards pierced your heart with sky magic and wrote love letters with rain, with tears reflecting your beautiful shining splendor through infinite shades of colored rainbow magic.

Shadows flow through shadows
Light through light
Wonderment ripples and surges into song that echoes your reflection on the waves beckoning you to dance. This life this life this dance this ballet pirouetting wings unfolding extending everywhere and nowhere into the empty spaciousness where forever and never collided.

Filigreed light shadows pouring over the moon lit sea. The fullness of emptiness sighs. nighthawks swoop and swirl in the shadow of the moonlight, and never catch the day

Moonlight weeps at its own reflection dancing across the rippling waves

In the kiss of night
Where darkness meets fullness
Radiance blossoms and falls
I could see the notes clearly
Hanging from ropes of twining space in the vast blueness
But I lost my eyes in the seeing of it
And there was only the vastness
Where memories played and danced across the mind screen
Where laughter and sorrow folded into the depths without time
there was an out breath
A hush
And ripples sparkled in the moon song that had no name

your breath my breath, wind beneath our feet, dancing as this warm
summer's breeze.
your tears my tears, wetness falling in, rushing torrents, lightly
skimming ripples
tears of no one
tears of no where
dissolved in kisses
tears uncounted un-named ocean saltiness
iridescent stillness
waving

nothing everything
shadows never kissing
melting songs of homelessness
and the loveliness of home

Like a song that you sang long ago but you have never heard
you cannot remember the words or the melody yet you can feel it
deeply.

Twirling twining echoed reflections dancing shimmering flowing
down the canyon Moonlight sings
And it sounds like love

only through each other's I's can we see ourselves, catch a glimpse
of our beauty
and your eyes are my eyes

we need a little imaginary separation in order to touch
in order to gaze into each other's beauty and say I love you

songs pour through me casting ripples as we are adrift on this
shoreless ocean
this sea of dreams
rudderless without anchor or place of shelter
oh! this unspeakable fluid ease of boundless vast pure
spaciousness
kissing endless sky
sun dancing liquid light
shimmering shadows calling hello goodbye hello
I offer rhythmic syllables that rock you gently
washing over you under you through you a caress of song

yet you who no longer search for a lullaby
know you will drown
You can feel the tsunami approach
Sea is rising
Sky is falling
Oceans of tears greet their salty home

No one said this would be easy
Having your world ripped asunder
Having you blood and guts and heart ripped out

But you wanted this
Remember
More than anything else
Here it is
It has always been here
Gently gnawing at your heart
There's no turning back now
There is no back
This is it, coyote

....and when all boundaries are dissolved there are no more empty
spaces that need to be filled...

Weeping laughing crying sobbing soaring flying streaming dancing twirling in delight

This utter vast clear spaciousness that we are pulled us into and through ourselves
unfolding infolding weaving unweaving endless cats cradles rocking falling
Spilling flying into explosions imploding wonderment
Sighing singing breathing us, dancing us in atemporal rhythmless rhythms
Strewn like stars across the night sky draped in love light spiraling effervescent luminescence rippling into and through itself

The sky burst open
Those imaginary pieces pierced what felt like a separate heart
Shards of mirrored blue
You saw your face in every one

Many seem to see through the illusion of self and believe that they are a person who has seen through the belief in self
So often they simply assume that they are awareness
It's like a bigger better me
The seeing that there are no things nor holder of them is exceedingly rare
One glimpse has the self looking for another reference point
ANY reference point
It's simply too dizzying
And fear laden

So many become fixated on the idea of something solid or stable or fixed and after seeing through the solidity of self simply grab onto another imaginary reference point called God or true self or source or timeless awareness
(Fill in the blank)
These are imaginary placeholders, like zero is used in mathematics, preventing your whole world from falling apart

However your tears may fill your foot falls and the edges will crumble
......words sliding into the desert dream

There is indeed a bittersweet sublime ache for life as it is
It is like the shimmering of a beautiful cold hard center-less
diamond
Revolving around the sun
basking in own reflected light and warmth

No special way to feel
Just looking and feeling like anything at all
How wondrous it is to feel
The rush the roar the zing of your beautiful aliveness

This is it coyote
Your one and only life
Your one and only brief moment
Except it is no longer yours
It never was

And I sing and sing and sing and the songs soar my imaginary lines
into the canyons
The rifts and valleys of this and that.... shadows breaking in the
summer sun

She wanted to bathe her heart in seamless sky......
clouds, she ran from ...and the rain.
Yet the rain continued inside
wetness merged with wetness
inside and outside kissed and slid through these sideless sides

dawn traipsed down the clouds blooming, colored hearts unfurled
within without ...where was that heart she had so longed to soothe?

it had fallen through the vastness
singing

joy and sorrow merged
and there was no one left to look for the crumbs left by birds in the
sparkling sky

Night
Swoops in
And grabs your lonely feet
Dawn is just a heartbeat away
Fear of the dark
Has lost its hold
Headlights mark your empty footsteps
Their rhyme and rhythm
Merges with the heartbeat of existence
Closer than close
Closer than the tongue in your mouth
Closer than thoughts or feelings
There was never a space between your heart and your head
Or the distant sky
And love

falling out of the picture leaving only overtones, like halos of
emptiness that side into and through each other erasing
themselves

through the mist
mountain tops
laughter reflects in cloudy sky
falling into my reflection
I hear the winds laughing
the receding waves sink into the sunlit sand
backwards tumbling
rainbows laughing
echoes dancing
sea of dreams
infinite permutations
colors dancing
reaching out sliding through
my own echo
hello
goodby
hello

Lightly tripling down the canyon caressing your heart strings

An echo dances
Calling you
Strangely familiar as it whirlpools around your roots and begins to
unfurl you unfold you into itself yourself
You try to run but your own love for the song submerges you in the
flowing and you drown in your own footsteps

echoed heart song
windswept beaches
empty dreams

simply this symphony of perception
fantastical kaleidoscopic light and sound show
falling through itself
you are the song of the canyon
caressing touching hearing itself
within its own echoes as it washes through rippling memories
Rushing roaring falling into its own sunset kiss

not two
not one
not neither
not both
not this nor that
not freedom
nor bondage...
no place left to land
no one who can
neither confusion
nor non-confusion
not light or dark
not location less or located
not up or down
nor lost or found
neither wet nor dry nor sun nor shade

here we are speaking of nothing
isn't that amazing
lines like filigreed percussions of emptiness
swirling into apparent thingness

reverberating echoes fill and empty your heart
resounding nothingness dissolved into itself
not even nothing to be found

snail creeps on the sidewalk
he may be crushed
only we know of death
only we know of life
only we know of this amazement
that blows us away
light melting into light
it puddles on the sidewalks and leaks into your being...
there is no barrier between you and your tears...
it was only thought
that seemed to obscure the brightness
it was only memory that seemed to create a path back to itself
The chorus of your own love song has never been hidden
it penetrates your dreams night and day, it can never be forgotten
for it is everything and nothing continually appearing and resolving
...falling into itself
And he looked up at the night sky and saw the stars
scattered ....magical beautiful
And then someone told him what the constellations were
he didn't feel quite the same way about the stars anymore…

I took a psychology class at and the professor asked one day who
out of the group of 300 would like to have their handwriting
analyzed
many raise their hands and many gave samples

The next day he passed out little pieces of paper to everyone who
had offered their handwriting, and asked everyone to raise their
hand if what they wrote on the paper seemed to be true. Almost
everyone raised their hands. Then he began reading from a piece
of paper from the podium. A low laughter began in the room as
everyone realized that they had received the exact same piece of
paper.

The idea that someone would want their future told.

I guess the longing for security can outweigh the longing for magic
Even when I believed in the future I never wanted to know it

Magical thinking keeps the self feeling safe. It was always the gnawing feeling deep down that there is nothing solid or stable or fixed, that the self is made up. There's a constant effort to fill in the holes fill in the blanks, to repair any breach in the imaginary walls of knowing and fear of unknowing

I see jewels everywhere
Where to put all this love?
No empty pockets
That need filling
No one separate from this love that seems to paint a reflection of me, that swoons with sky like wonderment as I see myself through your beautiful beautiful eyes

Infinite broken hearts sailing on a sea of joy
Seekers want to expand what they think of as their awareness or their consciousness. Can you find and outside or edge to awareness? Is it a thing? Is it separate from you? If there is no edge than there is no outside and there fore nothing outside of it.

What are its qualities and characteristics? If it has no edge is it a thing? Is awareness ever not present? Is there ever awareness without perception or observed without observer? Are they actually two things, or is it only words that make it seem like they are separate things, is it merely words that make it seem like there are things at all?

How could anything get in the way of being in the here and now?
There is really no here and now nor you to be in it or not in it.
Can you find the beginning and end to a thought or feeling or moment?
Are there separate thoughts feelings or moments?
Is there a you separate from thought feeling or this ever arising ever dissolving edgeless momentary?

What is going on is always this seamless uninterrupted flow without separate things or moments. There are no things yet all things are included. Including the idea that there is a separate you who can be in the here and now or not. All of life happens utterly spontaneously, and may include the dissolving of belief in belief.

Most teachers assume there is someone under the story
Some say let go of your story, perpetuating the belief that there is a permanent unchanging self who has a story or beliefs of thoughts or emotions.

Some say rest as awareness
Perpetuating the painful belief that awareness is a thing and so are you.

A someone who has a choice on how think feel or act
As if there is a person separate from thought feeling action
Or a right or wrong way to think feel or act
Or indeed separate thoughts feelings or actions
And there are not

Many will say you're already enlightened
Perpetuating the belief that enlightenment happens to the person
Then they will tell you how to realize that you are enlightened
Perpetuating the painful belief in a self with personal volition

And that's beautiful
It keeps the seeker safe
Only a few will see this inconsistency
And perhaps their brains will stop believing in the passion play it is painting
However this intellectual understanding is not required

As soon as the belief in separation settles in there is an ongoing ache, an all pervading loneliness, and a longing to feel whole and complete
Imaginary separation is never quite believed
It never feels right

With the arising of the illusory persona there is an accompanying fear of its demise.

So self cannot help but seek to patch the holes, to connect the dots, to glue together the pieces that were never separate. Most find the shelter of religion or spirituality, of gods or aliens to fend off the fear of the darkness that haunts them day and night.

Many seek solace in finding the clothes of more labels, of psychology astrology philosophy
More clubs to hold hands to try to feel safe
To find that ultimate shelter in the dark

But for some
The candle cannot fool them
They long for the bonfire
Most are the belief that there is someone doing life, choosing this or that, yet they seem not to be able to choose to not feel like the chooser.

Most are the belief that they are on a path.
To enlightenment or winning something
Usually some kind of place of rest
Wealth or retirement or simply understanding
Sitting under a palm tree with a glass of something that has a little umbrella in it.
Or heaven
Or their next life when they can finally get it right

As the feeling of self begins to take form, the belief in separation begins to cut the world into imaginary pieces. Especially all that is me...
And all that is not
All the pieces have sharp edges that hurt deep inside
There is a vague memory of being just the big wow. There may be a feeling of loss as that knowingness of seamless ease starts to fade as anxiety and fear begin.
The feeling of separation is extraordinarily painful for some
They become spiritual seekers

It seems I was always having glimpses yet I never attributed it to some kind of God
The knowing feeling of pure seamless vastness never felt like it was coming from a source outside of myself

So many have a glimpse of life doing itself and believe that someone else is doing it, or that it's somehow predetermined.
Written in the stars
Or god planned.

Before the shift I used to love to watch the tree tops dance in the wind
Sparkling shine and shade singing in the sun
Now that the feeling of inside outside is gone
I am the wind and the light and the shimmering flowing through me as me

A whoosh of love seemingly takes flight and creates hearts with wings that soar and tumble and sigh a love song like this. In love as love through love, yet there is no love nor anyone to love or be loved.
We are winged sailing ships on a sea of dreams.

Perfection in one
Perfection in two
Perfection in many
Oneness swallows twoness swallows oneness
the dream of I am exploded into the dream of we are

all the words ever uttered will not unlock the sky
not until an ocean of tears is ripped out of your chest will the heavens kiss endless seas and blueness flow through you as you

clouds form themselves streaming blossoming blooming across the blueness
mind of this and that
the lens of self
sees images faces stories
Born of memories

...of descriptions ideas abstractions learned from others
all the ideas that we grabbed in our desperation
this overwhelming fear
pretending that we would not die, that our lives meant something,
that we had a purpose.

The stories un-write them selves as the winds are always blowing,
and we find new ones, softer ones, more comfortable ones, easy
chairs in the sky.

We may see that it is a house of cards. Trees grown in air.

and I sing and I sing and I sing and I sing of this sublime edgeless-
ness, yet every word seems to cut up the sky. Even this song itself
seems to trace a path... wake-less iridescence streams across the
vastness

that has no word

that has no echo

that has no melody

only a pure tone unhindered unfathomable
reaching
everywhere and no where

hearts stretch out to kiss what cannot be kissed...

it cannot be captured
it cannot be rounded out or squared
or changed or pounced upon or gathered up
or added to or subtracted from
if I could I would grab you and kiss you long and deep
and penetrate your very being with my deep un-wavering
knowingness of total perfection

Suspended as nothingness and soaring naked simultaneously

a flying dream, a scintillating chorus of one, touching breathing caressing itself. Swooning forever into your own infinite intimate embrace.

What was it that broke the mirror
And ripped you to shreds as you fell through.

It was your own reflection
Weeping

She watched as words blossomed into colors and shapes and imaginary lines twisted and turned into this flowing garden of infinite things, as rainbows showered luster into an inside and painted flowers into an outside
An intimate caress of shadows dancing
Light filled the inky blackness
Deep green-y blues sparkled in the depths where primordial darkness surged into the rising sun and rippled into songs
Tales of passion
Lives of sorrow and joy
All swirling into and through each other
Descending into the dusk

It is brief and precious beyond measure
More wondrous than words can kiss

Songs reflect the moonlit dance
and twirl and sparkle in lover's eyes.
but they never touch or capture even a scent of the wondrousness.

rippling
flowing
through all and everything
and nothing

and thunder roars in your veins
it is the sea
boiling

this vibrancy
this tsunami of unfettered life
falling rushing through you
moves you
dances you
sings the song of you

when the center the tight knot the bewildering terrifying assumption
that you are doing it
is ripped open
the roller coaster of hope and fear jumps the tracks

and there is sailing with no need to grasp the tiller or man the sails
it was an illusion that you had to go somewhere
or that there was somewhere to go
or that there was anyone who could go
anywhere
or nowhere

and the sun and moon slide across the sky
and stars sparkle so
rainbows flow through you as you
when your shadow is no longer in the way

the passion play writes itself in the sky and never leaves a trace to
read
we are snapshots of sky writing
cloud reflections rippling through pristine natural stillness
a dance unlike any other
empty footfalls crumbling

She thought she had to watch the clouds forming disappearing
weaving thought dreams in the sky
Or watch the birds streaming sweeping swooping circling spiraling
touching resting on tall tree tops dancing in the wind.

Her lines were the parameters where she thought she could find
beauty

Special thoughts special emotions special places to rest her attention

A certain lovers kiss

A special time of day
the magic hour
or early dawn

Or walking in a gentle rain, the beautiful sound of the drops on her umbrella and the magical light from within from without merging touching swooning into her through her as her

And the longing for life to be a certain way began to consume her, the longing for this love.

This shock of recognition of total and complete perfection.

So she tried to stop to capture the magic knowing deeply and fearfully however deep down that the magic was in the flowing was in the impermanence.

Rippling reflections flowing over and under and into and through each other, enchanting bewitching transfixing.

The desire became like a heartache
Would it ever be fulfilled… she began to realize it could not

The longing itself was the beauty her beauty shining brilliantly

and what she feared for so long begin to reveal itself
In every teardrop

All sight all sound
all emotion all thought
All touch......
all sensation

there never was someone to grasp it
or hold it or treasure it

this edgeless streaming flowing un-capture-able unknowable vast
pure spacious sky like brilliance
doing itself
had pierced her consumed her with it's undeniable magnificence

and spit her out
her new clothes loosely worn starlight dancing
Gossamer wing'd awe
It's really beyond imagination
This is beyond ideas of emptiness beyond ideas of nothingness
beyond ideas of enlightenment beyond ideas of
Beyond...
There are no things to be joined and there is no thing to be
separated

There are no things or non-things yet everything is included

A double twist Möbius strip

A deja vu within a deja vu

There are no things to be joined and there is no thing to be
separated

The heart is made up
Like love
Like you
Brain thinks you
You are not the thinker
you are an illusion
you are a dream
not the dreamer

You are an illusion
you are made up
you are imagined
that is beyond imagination

There is sublime melancholy in this beautiful aloneness. I find it everywhere and nowhere, it speaks to me and sings me in tear'd reflections of unbearable beauty.

I sit in the sun crocheting as the dream crochets me into the sun. My hands, rainbow yarn, life weaving itself magically. The soft sound as my husband sands his wooden cabinet showering suspended dust sparkling in the afternoon sun catching on the cobwebs woven into ivy. Sun gently caressing the canyon, soft footfalls, cracks in the sidewalk, trees aching to kiss the sky.

The tsunami that crushed the sky folded me into its arms until every tear blended into seamless blue.

tattered sails, shredded dreams fill empty blue with shades of midnight. memories of tears coalesce and wash through me and paint an unspeakable dream that magically sings color and light that echo just like this. this heart breaking-ly wondrous life.

a deep hush wove itself into the dream
and has never left

You are love's smile gazing upon itself
Always the first and last kiss
Of all and everything
Forever and never
Emptiness flows
Uncontainable unadorned naked
Love breathes
You are we are this is
Unbearably wondrous

All unutterably perfect
Nothing out of place
When there are no things

you can find yourself only in the love-light of other's reflections
Whilst endless after images shimmer in future moon-glow caught in the rippling past
Never held or captured
A mirage of untold beauty

Where suns and moons and misty dreams played upon shadowy
dancers who spiraled together in infinite wonderment
A dream
yes
Magnificent
yes
Pierced by joy and sorrow
Sucked into a black hole
Exploding into everywhere
And no where

And the ache the longing for this richness this lushness this magic
carpet of bejeweled wonder, multidimensional iridescence
showering memories into a bottomless bucket that rain color
through your beautiful eyes.

It is your heart-song
No one sings it
It sings you

wings lift and ease in the blooming of wind
dancing shimmering palm fronds
painting traceless designs on the sand
rippling kissing fading foot prints
the lostness of a place to rest is bittersweet
yet no longer looking is sublime

skimming reflections
gazed sideways
The fullness of emptiness flows though the weight of its own
effulgence
Shadows shimmering
Beyond nothing or everything
past any idea of two lips touching
real kisses happen
Wings of nothing dipped in rainbows paint your heart in sky

slipping endlessly into beauty
Simultaneously falling and bursting into stars singing endless love
songs into vastness

Transparent and yet vividly apparent, this precious jewel that you are is the very emptiness that allows for endless reflections. The me reflecting as you which feels like the most sublime love.
And brilliant diamonds slide down the empty streets...

Life as a human being is filled with great sorrow and unutterable joy

One brief shining tear
Through which life catches a glimpse of its own majesty and mystery feeling touching seeing wondering at its own magnificent aliveness

Wheels on cobblestone
Rushing headlights
Motors dancing

Palm fronds sliding repetition in the shadows like a piano playing a duet with itself

Its always been a player piano
No fingers ever touched a key
the melody
so sublime
wraps around you through you in you
it has always been you

Joy and sorrow are indistinguishable

Without labels
this seamless smoothness
felt deeply
tears still flow
waves of unowned emotion
Skimming delicate beauty

We recognize beauty as we are beautiful
But there is no one to capture it
Oneness swallows twoness swallows oneness
Perfection in one

Perfection in two
Perfection in many

All felt deeply simultaneously
The whoosh falling through the whoosh

Iridescence swirling infinite colors merging spinning dancing without
edges singing overtones of deeply felt hues and uncountable stars
flooding through their eyes

Spinning infinitely into each other's emptiness and fullness
Starlight dancing

Swooningintotheswoon

You long to fall and be held, yet when you reach the edge of the
known world, ideas and concepts, the dream of this and that and
here and there,
there's a great void
You don't exist there.

There is no here nor there.
there's a great emptiness beyond all concepts of emptiness.
there's a great nothingness beyond all concepts of nothingness.
there's no non-place where there are no things to be understood or
not understood
and there is no you to understand or not understand them.

Sea foam clouds erupt into blueness and rush across the sky.
Tumbling and growing darker and darker.
rain softens the air
where seabirds hang

There has never been any one at the helm
there has never been a steering wheel
there is never been a prow of a ship going somewhere
all there is is a shoreless ocean
This sea of dreams

You may feel dizzy

Or confused
Until you realize there is no one to be confused or non confused

The wall of fear dissolves. Your heart drops. It was never yours.
You know there is no next... there is no past...

You know you cannot do or not do anything. You have never been
separate from what's going on. What lies in-between you and this
inseparable momentary? There is not even nothing, as thought is
this seamless brilliant immediacy also.

There is nothing outside of this.
Everything is included
Where else could it possibly be?

You have always been naked
I recognize your nakedness
As it is mine

Simply this, of itself so.
Sea of sighs
filled with tears
reflecting unseen rainbows
in our beautiful beautiful eyes

Liquid Eyes Of Love

tattooed with smiles and tears
nothing underneath my nakedness
no one wears the stars
or sunlight dancing
garden path
has no wanderer
echoes bloom
thought weaves a thinker
spider web catches the last light
day falls into the cats cradle
of dark

Plunged into the sea of unknowing
Still, wind and light play on the surface
No overarching truth
Only sky and sea
Sun and moon and stars
No words can contain this light
That has no questions
Or answers
No empty pages need be filled
With the petals of today

Colors cascade down the canyon
Echo on the walls
Slide into your footsteps
Sing these flowers blooming
Dance these winds through your shadow
Explode your very heart
That the ink washed through
That wrote the tales of last summer's love songs
That etched your twirling silhouette into sky

This sensuous lostness
Of wind and sun and sky
Soaring skinless
Bathed with color and primordial melodies
That sing these very words

Walking through morning
Light pours me
Inside out

Pirouette of mirrors
Love recognizes itself
Infinite facets of my own reflection
Eviscerate the illusion
Of solidity

This clear fluidity
Drinks me
I soar through this vast unknowable unknown
Without wings
Or any place to land

no words....
So many words
Spring blossoms and falls
Scattering velvet petals among our footfalls
That no one can follow or grasp or trace, even memory flows along
the river that we drowned in long ago far away when we lost the
belief that we were unchanging
Wind sings our name
Our name is love
It beckons us
It is us

It's a bittersweet beautiful melancholy
Time
Life

Sadness
Joy
Awe
Happen
For no one
To no one
Yet I'm here
Sobbing

Emptiness a word to try to swallow the ocean
Consciousness another to try to calm the sea
Truth an idea, an imaginary port on these edgeless waters
God a concept to try to hide
Your naked aloneness
The ever looming horizon
Sunset beckons...

I see your brokenhearted beauty
Through these eyes that are not mine
Through these lips these teeth this tongue
These words that we share sing themselves
This edgeless momentary that burns itself
Is the fire of your aliveness

Slip stream of life
Wind
My empty breath
Flower of moon
Falls through this open hand

Drinking deeply this softness
Falling petals paint the tapestry of wind
Flowing through itself

Glass casts its own shadow
Illuminates your reflection

Dissolves as you swallow
Life as it swallows you.

Wind blows
Hearts beat and brake
Rain and tears fall
Gathering in pools of echoes that shimmer in their own reflection.

For no reason the moon rises and shadows of memory flow across
the leaf scattered path.
That no one followed
That no one danced upon.
Yet you find yourself dancing with the darkness and the sliver of
ancient moon.

The garden a stage where we seem to meet in the birth of night
touching day,
In between sky
We no longer look for shadows under the wind's gathering of
leaves from autumn.
No more dreams to burn...

Winter clothes itself with tears
It's nakedness reaches up through the long silence.
Love melts the shadows of ice crystals flowing.
The darkness was never empty
Nor full
You could no longer hide from your own shadow or your own
beautiful reflection.
It burnt its name in your heart
That you treasured
For awhile,
Until the vastness claimed itself.
Spring grew into summer and time flowed back into and through
itself.

Where is the beginning and end of sky
When sky is your nakedness

Your aloneness
The majesty
That no one wears

Drowned dissolved as the sea of edgeless beauty, my sourceless reflection soars over the billowing ripples of love's sacred melody echoing the heartbeat of one of two of many of none.
Under this rainbow raiment of a poet's song, behind these liquid eyes of love, beneath this naked unadorned sky like wonder there is not even nothing at all.
There's not something inside us which loves so deeply.
It is who we are.
You don't have wonder, you are wonder itself.
You don't know beauty, you are beauty itself.
You can't know love, you are love itself.

I am the reaching out to touch knowing there is no touching.
I am the midnight love song fading in the morning mist.
I am the embrace of the river weeping at its own wetness.
I am the ache of nothing melting into these very words that slide across your mind stream and fabricate fairy tales of a beautiful waltz, a pas de deux, a syncopated beat rippling through the farthest reaches of your memory knocking on the doors to a knowing feeling that this life this life this beautiful life has no rhythm no rhyme no meaning nor non meaning nor any one to have it...

I am the longing to catch life in a bottle and send it to you so you can press this opalescent shell to your ear and hear the seas sing your name.
Life calls you, beckons you to dance beyond these words, yet there is not even nothing behind the curtain, or underneath your magnificent tears, no one loving this love.

Drinking deeply this life that you have longed for and feared has been drinking you. It has always been your beautiful iridescence that crashed into itself on parallel lines fading into the distance.
They could never meet, as they were never apart. We could never meet as we have never been apart.
I am the reaching out to touch knowing we can never touch.

This touch-less touch of your own embrace.

the film unwinds itself
celluloid transparency
painted on both sides
nothing in the middle
erases the sides

no pictures caught in this wave
reflecting day above
dark below
kissed in between the wet
you drown in your own echo
sea shells worn with the rush and ebb of tides
reveal your seamless beauty
sea bird flies through cloud and sun
shadows drink the day
this sensuous lostness
pathless land
kisses you
where never and forever collide

I spied my reflection in the garden pond, my hair bedecked with
fallen leaves, golden greens wet with sky hovering over the
deepness. This penetrating beauty cannot see itself, even in
daylight. In the depths of midnight the unfathomable nature of love
beckons your heart to fall to plummet to swoon into its empty echo,
as love needs edges to fall through itself.

A great wind sweeps through me and it is me, fills me empties me,
and the cat sleeps unaware of her beauty.

There are no words for wordlessness. Yet... my thumb taps the
glass and songs flow…
Shattered mirrors of smiles form rivulets for tears. There is no light
without dark.
No one wants to hear about their ultimate emptiness, their ultimate
aloneness. Yet for some, this beautiful naked unadorned life, the
starkness of emptiness dancing beckons.

Enchanted with the magic of not knowing, of not being able to swallow infinite blue, your heart explodes as you dissolve into the kiss of liquid sky.

The wet of wet, the taste of taste, inside and out, lose their sides and there is no one left to win. Trackless unowned memories reflect your delicate fingerprints as they fade in the dusk. Breathtakingly ravishingly unfathomable, unspeakable. Emptiness unwound your seamless borders and unraveled all ideas that seemed to separate you from deep deep sorrow and unspeakable joy. You were everything and nothing at all. Simultaneously everywhere and nowhere.

Drinking your shadow as it swirls in this empty bottomless sideless cup it overflows in a love dance as it swallows you utterly and completely.

You are the love poem that echoed in the distant canyon that summer's eve when you first discovered how to dance. That mournful feeling when you took your first step. That beautiful sorrow when love died. That smile that seems to weep without end. The sublime heartache of knowing you are nothing but an ephemeral thought dream and all whom you have ever loved nothing more than a midnight kiss that have blazed your heart with tattoos of infinite faces, of countless sorrows, of unfettered joy, and sings this intimate song that sings you.

Edgeless fluidity streams without movement, sings without sound, yet it is heard as it echoes in the depths of your being. Closer than close, closer than your heart beat, closer than love, it is profoundly felt as it dances you. You realize you are a tattered day dream, and there is no it, no nothing, no everything, no emptiness.. You are not close nor far as even placeless-ness dissolves into the paper cup that is dissolving in your very drinking of these words that seem to capture the aliveness you feel.

This has no words, and includes all words, as the beauty of this naturally occurring magnificence floors you, knocks your socks off and leaves you breathless. All and everything is known to be a water color day dream dissolving into its own wetness, its own colors swallow themselves in their thirst to dance.

Untraceable super perfection is exquisite in its ambiguousness, and obvious when there is no finger upon the rim of your glass trying to catch the music that streams from its own reflection. Yet the finger is perfection itself, for where would you be without a point of view? There never was a moon in your cup nor its reflection, nor a glass to catch it, nor hands nor heart to hold it. You drink deeply as moonlight beckons in this ecstatic love dance that swirls again as you tip your glass and watch your reflection kiss itself. Beauty reveals itself like this.

Amidst the hustle and bustle she heard the strains of her heart song and the slow dance began. She held out her gloved hand for the last waltz and fell through her partner through herself into her own embrace. The dance floor fell away…
The great hall dissolved into space…
She was the music and the dance and the wind silently breathing utterly sublimely bittersweetly alone

Midnight winds eased down the canyon
Teasing a loose shutter
To sing its song everyone recognized
But no one could follow
A heartbeat
Without rhythm or rhyme
An ache of a memory
Bled into the vastness
A shadow danced
There were not even bones
That rattled
Love's magic pierced your heart as sea rose up and smashed into sky and crushed you utterly.
Your smile your teeth your skin your lips your tongue your blood your heart the very innermost core of your being exploded imploded and love bled into the dream. You found you are the sky and the rainbow, light dancing with itself, the treasure the beauty the magic you had longed for.

Sunset waves reflect your tears, sea kissing sky kissing sea. Drowning in each other's echoed love songs bathed in your own beauty, swallowed by your infinite smile, washed away in fields of rippling shine and shadow.

Your heart was never hidden at the end of the rainbow. It exploded into infinite perfection and you have never lost it, as it was never yours.

It was only the idea that it was separate from you that formed you and made you a seeker of your own love.

Tears echo your flowing iridescence falling softly on a hot summers night reminding you of your precious humanness, bathed in your own nakedness.

We are watercolor thought dreams painted in pure space echoing madly the song of the universe.

...and what is the kiss of emptiness weeping at its own beauty....

He stood on the edge of the precipice, starlight flooding his nakedness and he wondered if his lovers had ever existed. He wondered if love was also a dream? The Nighthawk swooped, its shadow over whelmed him, as he stared into the void and the void stared back.

...what is the sound of one heart weeping...

All thingness, including you, is like an iridescent swirling that pretends to separate the space inside of a bubble from the outside. When believed in it is like a felt tension a constriction both physically and mentally.

Truth and reality are ideas. What is going on is edgeless seamless fluid, neither moving nor non-moving, and cannot be caught with the razor of thought.

Like a snapshot description, a butterfly pinned, all thingness is dead. What could possibly capture this symphony of ever moving perception?

For it is infinite, the breath the footsteps the sounds the tastes the colors, the formless forms, patternless patterns, rhythmless rhythms, more intimate than you're very breath, then your tongue in your mouth.

This is all we ever wanted and yet it was nothing at all. Searching for what had never left yet had never been.
You will follow an empty dream until it unfolds itself dropping you through a rabbit hole with no end or beginning. Until the falling is falling, and there is no more wish to grab the magic. The magic is you, and it is everywhere and no where… center-less jewels everywhere sparkling shimmering baseless reflections…
All echoing a shared dream ricocheting down an endless canyon where love dies.
Hello goodbye hello…
We are the impossible beauty of love's simultaneous blooming and wilting.

From every direction from no direction wordless songs written unwritten unheard unsung gather exploding imploding countless tears blasting space into infinite mirrored reflections.
…like a still rippling sliding flowing hush reflecting dancing sourceless starlight from inside and out…
from everywhere from nowhere rushing silence roaring flooding soaring tip toeing ever blooming ever wilting softly merging quiescence never separate or joined singing whirl-pooling waving flowing tapestried wonder. Tender filigreed tears shimmer in this kaleidoscopic dream land as watercolor kisses hum a song of you.

We need our imaginary lines otherwise we cannot touch or kiss or dance. They are constantly writing themselves. I love watching my lines form, and love flow.
I step out into the night, cricket song engulfs me, tires rolling, engines punctuates the hush.

You always knew this, in the hush before dawn, and you always felt it. As you gazed helpless into the sunset emerged submerged subsumed in the colors in the light in the shadow. No longer trying to count the stars you fell into sky …where was the space between you and sadness... Whose tears slid down these cheeks?
As the sun and moon slide across the vault of your aching heart, time dies. Trying to peer under the night swallowed by starlight,

drenched in a canopy of tears holding an empty prize, you dissolved into wonder.

The record spins and you are the needle and the groove and the song. It is always your song, it always has been.
...and what is it that words cannot touch ...what is it that we cannot know... what is it that cannot be pushed or pulled or added to or taken away from or analyzed or taken apart... or thought about ....or figured out ...or boxed in or boxed out or accepted or rejected... what is this aliveness this vividness that is felt so deeply... so profoundly ..it contains all and everything yet is limitless ... all pervasive all encompassing ...never not here or there ...appearing as everything... thing-less untouchable sublime edgeless-ness...
....unknowable ....it cannot see itself... when you stop trying to grasp it you disappear...

Clutching your invitation to the dance, the music stopped, the floor dropped out, turned inside out your gut wrenched free. As all the tendrils of belief untied themselves.
Nothing you had counted on remains, all the places you used to hide were gone.
All ideas are seen to be baseless echoes that created imaginary meaning out of a sigh inseparable from wind.

The house of cards, the castle in the sky, collapses when it's all recognized to be hearsay.
A crumpled empty dance card sailing in the wind.
We are imaginary beings living in an edgeless sea of dreams. A magic show a trick of the tale, a hologram a pseudo-reality, a virtual reality of separate things and separate events. Where trees stretch their branches into the vast sky and push their roots deep into the earth.   Where lovers meet silently in pools of light on the sidewalk. Laughter in the distance echoes in the canyon, the last partygoers wander home chatting excitedly about the day, and the evening, and their hopes for tomorrow.

When one of the characters loses all hope and fear, they are like an empty shadow a ghost amongst the living. All they see is perfection everywhere and in everyone. They cry a lot and say, 'I love you you, are beautiful.'

Being is longing… Even for just this… Like love like awe like heartache like, well, truly it's not like anything at all, is it, and yet we know it deeply because we are it.
What is there underneath the longing, that ache? There is no one who wears desire.
No need to get rid of desire or self, and that's good because you can't! You are not separate from these. This flow of life that has no edges, this river of song that sings you sings me sings love into the rippling of its own wetness.

I'm just sitting here silently watching my thumb seem to create words and images. Precious gems brilliantly slip into each others mind streams. Light starting to illuminate the back yard, and yet hours before the sun hits here in this narrow canyon. I am sublimely immersed in the warm liquidity of home, basking in this oceanic warmth as dolphins play in the mind stream, jumping, bursting into the air the sun the light, innumerable rainbow droplets falling into the sparkling see... ripples flowing leading nowhere, and falling back into myself never having gone anywhere.

Spinning madly twirling echoes resounding from everywhere and nowhere, I was looking for the origin of time and was lost in a web of words. Like space seemed to be trapped inside a spider web, the filigreed design catching the light so beautifully, dancing in the wind. Swooning into the spin, the radiating wonder was me. Never caught, never held, it's obviousness seemed to obscure it.
Searching for meaning gave a false sense of solidity to life.
Where was my last step?
Ricocheting delight and awe, empty footfalls dance with the weight of light streaming from sourceless wonder.
Weightless, riding the wind, a sigh a song, a seabird flies by, you can see his shadow on the water, brilliant shimmering dancing in

the waves. Slipping into the sea, rainbows on the surface reflect rainbows on the bottom sand. Can't tell which way is up, drowned, Breathing underwater, dissolved into the ocean of love. Every pore of my being is awash, flooded, Insane with awe…
And the wlnd whips around your ears and you lean into the storm as you are the storm and it's empty center, and walk on.

Sometimes a mountain stream leaps and gurgles over the rocks and sometimes it passes through the most lovely grassy clearings where the deer come to drink and there's a most beautiful hush.

You look back. You remember so many events that seemed to be leading somewhere, and you know they were just part of the show. The illusion of someone on a path going... what was it that she wanted? It's seen that the cause of anything is everything, and as there are no things, the cause of everything is …nothing. Really all trying to connect the imaginary dots simply stops.

Unconditional love is knowing there are no things and no you to be separate from them. It's the knowing feeling of seamlessness. It's the knowing that you are ultimately alone and that all imaginary others also feel this great heartache of their great aloneness. Feeling deeply that you exist only as reflections in another's beautiful eyes, this love is like reflections of love dancing, echoing reverberating the heartbeat of existence into the marvelous song of you of me of we.
This is like love but unlike any ideas of love.

Haven't you ever put on a sad song and listened to it over and over and over again and reveled in kind of a beautiful sweet sorrow? Perhaps memories of old lovers or friends or parents or your past, now gone, or a generalized sorrow, the sorrow of the ages of everyone who has ever loved. The beautiful heart ache of being human.
The feeling of the preciousness of this life, this fleeting brief life, a feeling of the preciousness of love, of being able to feel so deeply, even sorrow.

Bewitched entranced by the shimmering you reached to touch it to grasp it to hold it and you fell into and through your own reflection. The words slid off your timeline as you fell through the mirror laughing and weeping.

When the cage of adornment shatters, all that's left is wide open spaciousness. You hear its echoing bells of laughter lighting up the endless reaches where stars cannot touch. As oceans of rainbows pour through you as you, they illuminate your heart and radiate outward and the dream is drenched in awe.

Space dissolves into itself, it swallows you whole as you drink deeply this unspeakable magic, and everywhere you look is your own heart your own smile your own love your own unsigned tears. You are drunk on the fathomless draft of life.

Laughter echoes in the canyon and you fall into the stars, your empty pockets have been ripped inside out and overflow with blazing light dancing. Imploding exploding light and darkness, forever and never, outside and in, and where they meet where they kiss is you. You are the winds rippling in the grasses and the waving dancing shine flowing into shadow and emerging again. Flowing description paints this utter splendor and sings you into existence

Not even emptiness, this merging of opposites, the sublime brilliant immediacy of this recognition that there were never any separate things to join, that you are this center-less jewel.

There never were sides, inside and and out, there never were directions or here or there. There never was time, a past or future or a now. Falling into and through this blooming wilting flowing scintillating aliveness, this seamless obvious beauty. Swimming soaring skinless as naked spacious sky. Sunlight starlight moonlight the wind moving rushing dancing through you as you. You are the shining the wind this ease of life itself.

I am this nakedness and there is nothing and no one wearing it.

And he clung to nothing and he clung to emptiness and he clung to mystery and he clung to ineffable and he clung to unknowing and he clung to unbelievable and he clung to meaninglessness.

And he clung to the idea that this was just a dream.

But it was simply beyond belief or understanding that he was indeed the dream and not the dreamer. He was the clinging, he could not let go. He was the grasping which substantiated the idea of a grasper and something to grasp.

For if there was no line between inside and outside, how could he keep all this love he was so afraid to feel and yet so longed to lose? What would happen if the damn holding back a lifetime of tears were to release itself?

What if indeed he were not the chooser of his thoughts and feelings?

What if indeed there were only thoughts and feelings, and he was a flowing thought dream?

What indeed if life was not like anything at all?

What indeed if life was only like itself?

The more words he discovered that seemed to give life meaning carved his silhouette with knives. Oh my! The imaginary line between inside and outside between this and that got scribbled in heavier and heavier and heavier and heavier like a noose cutting off all the light and love he longed for, but could never quite grasp. He tried to look between the lines and squiggles of the words, behind the sentences and ideas that he was. Just underneath the spinning skirts of the gypsy dream..

He could not find anything…

Not even nothing…

There is a great sense of loss and a deep deep mourning for yourself and for the belief in the dream, and belief in others, as that hole in your heart you had tried to fill explodes and implodes and you find there is not even nothing.

No longer trying to fill the emptiness it overflows with a bittersweet melancholia of joy and sorrow and awe and love that merge into a wondrous deep felt flow of emotion that is no longer owned, these naked tears are no longer counted or named. Such love of this dance no matter how it seems to appear.

All exceedingly intimate this knowing of no separation and this knowing that we exist only as imaginary separate selves. The knowing that under this unadorned nakedness there is not even

nothing. The longing to sing to touch to kiss is what defines the self. This beautiful heart ache I tried to escape is who I am.
You know this. You feel it deeply. This unwritten uncontrived unfettered undone un begun uninterrupted indivisible symphony... Magic... Pure magic!
You can taste it, feel it. It's on the tip of your tongue!
How long have you been searching for the words the syntax the rhythm the timing?
Echoing your dreams etching your heart with a longing an ache that you cannot describe?
Looking to capture it seems to obscure it.
You cannot have it. You are it.

I reached out my hands to hold the sky and the sky swallowed me.
I tried to dig my toes into the depths to penetrate the wonder, and earth and sea devoured me.
Kissed awake by awe itself, it slips on its diaphanous light gown that I am. Soaring as this shoreless sea of unutterable beauty extending infinitely in every direction without direction without movement or non movement, utterly obvious seamless ease.
Lying in bed gazing at the ceiling. Friends desperately recounting their stories of hope and fear. Walking in nature, in the market, catching people's I's, cooking dinner, sitting... tapping into my phone..
It's all so... All so.... Oh my! Indescribably marvelous!
Vibrantly alive this measureless existence unrhymed unowned, these tears I once felt separate from slide down these tender cheeks lined with rivulets of stars. Winged arabesques of flowing fleeting dragon tongues, whirls and swirls of untraceable wonder... Life never captured unleashes the simple joy of being.
I sing of darkness and I sing of light and every word seems to place a line in the sky. I sing of love and I sing of sadness and I sing of freedom and I sing of imaginary bonds that seem to choke us off, away, lost, forgotten, the utter sadness of trying to remember what cannot be forgotten, merely ignored.
Every morning it reappears as I flood into the lamplights like an unfathomable gem, thought sings me into the sparkling.

Awareness a name the objectifying brain gives to the recognition of perception, seemingly dividing the seamless indivisible symphony of life. Being aware of being aware is uniquely human. It's marvelous beyond compare to recognize and delight in its own delightedness. That we can wonder at the mystery of awe, and love the majesty of the unknowability and beauty of love.

Within the edgeless seamless sameness, this vast unspeakable magnificent expanse, emptiness overflows, colors begin to swirl, formless forms begin to swing themselves into patternless patterns, a-temporal contrapuntal rhythmless rhythms begin to dance and pirouette, waltzing flowing pouring light into light into streaming rainbow vibrant aliveness. Wordless wonder bursts into song A symphony of one, of infinite hue and timbre, overtones of silence wraparound and fold into and through them selves. Shine and shadow kiss all apparent thingness into a voice a song that sings itself.

without reason or no reason without a dance floor without rehearsal without a ticket to the dance you are the invitation the window, the brief portal, the infinite prism, the transparent magic lens breathing love and beauty into the universe vast wild and free beyond imagination this life this life this life this life... Oh oh oh oh!!!!!!

You are it, this kiss of madness, this song without words. A lovers kiss falling effortlessly into placeless unplanned unutterably supreme measureless magnificence!
Wide eyed
Twisting twirling shadows dancing
Ringlets of awe
Drenched with dew
Morning sings like this
Falling reflections of mirrored wonder
Simply the wind dancing In love with its own movement
Watching the leaves of unwritten stories fly away...
flowing bits of memory and pictures of tomorrow that no one drew. Mountain stream does not shimmer or sing without a listener. A river needs its banks to flow. Love requires imaginary twoness, a dance of one in love with itself.

What's going on prior to thought? Is there ANYTHING prior to thought? Is there even a prior? Before and after are thought created, aren't they?
Is there nothing or emptiness, or not even nothing?
Life is not even fluid, as until the symphony of perception is described there are no things to be permanent or changing. Is there actually movement or non movement without thought describing it? This is inconceivable, as it's not even an it until thought names it. Ungraspable, unspeakable, without any qualities or characteristics or dimension or time.
Even these words as you read them are painting thought tendrils that feel like they are reaching and capturing this vast unknowable unknown, painting sky flowers that are only attached to other thoughts, that paint other imaginary things.
All thought, learned shared words concepts ideas are constantly painting the dream of this and that, the dream of separation.
Only through thought can we seem to 'know' things.
Only through thought do we seem to appear.
So truly there are no separate things or non things that can be glued together into some kind of place of rest or understanding. There is no separate you who can grasp or understand what's going on, who can step outside of it and manipulate it accept it or reject it or surrender to it.
I cannot and am not trying to convince you that there are no things nor moments nor you, as awakening is NOT a belief or understanding or a philosophy or a set of rules to live by. It cannot be taught or learned or given away.

Clouds trying to grasp clouds.
Wind trying to hold wind.
Sun trying to capture its own warmth and light.
Hopes and dreams like forgotten fairy tales disappeared when fear flew out the window.
Starlight cannot kiss itself.
All these ideas about what enlightenment is supposed to be, all expectations running like a mantra….
Looking for words to fill in the blank.
Forever rebuilding repairing that wall of fear of unknowing…
Painting the window with a picture of how its supposed to be
Forever shutting out life and love…

rose petals falling
echo the wind
color the soft song of summer

breath of moonlight
sings of morning's slumber
in this garden
winter sleeps

under the shadow
no one gathers light
it pools by itself
drinking the day

It takes many years for us to really believe in the illusion of
separation, yet it is not entirely believed… that is why we feel this
lack… that there is something missing, and society says, 'yes, you
are flawed, and if you do this and this you will have well being.' Of
course all the things you are asked to do are impossible, (Have
only 'good' thoughts...love everyone...etc.)
We feel even more inadequate. It must be our fault! Happiness lies
somewhere in the future, our ideas of perfection may differ but we
all have some idea of what it would be and COULD be, and so we
are consumed with chasing that ever receding horizon, feeling that
we will someday get that golden goodie.
Because we feel woefully inadequate we take on the idea that
others know more about this than we do. Here comes religion,
psychology, philosophy and the guru. It's like we were shattered
into a million pieces and we are using these teachings to try to glue
the pieces together.
We seek until we don't. We ARE the seeking.

The idea that you are living in a body is a common misconception,
that you are an unchanging, awareness or consciousness or a spirit
or soul.
No body no brain no thoughts no you, as you are product of the
thought stream that arises from the brain. You are a flowing
thought dream. All thingness is the dream of objectified separation.

We can only know or see "things" and they are imaginary, like us. It may feel like you're a solid stable unchanging self or not. Awakening is the dream as well. We are the dream.

Love breaks free and fills utter emptiness with a song you had sung long ago, whose words you always longed for, always on the top of your tongue, yet could never quite remember, and you could never forget this longing.

Infinity arrayed iridescent shards of midnight pierce your very being, deeper than your heart, your love, your very life. A sublime crystalline matrix of this and that woven into an dream amplifies and breaks open the light into this utter magnificence. It grabs you and rakes you and shakes you apart at the seams, losing yourself in directionless center-less iridescence everywhere, nowhere.

There are no reference points whatsoever, no edges no center no corners left to hide in, no one left to hide. No one looking for succor, utterly naked raw, ripped inside out.. astonishing! The sheer wonder blows you away…

The scent after the spring rains fills the barren ground, promises of newness no longer sought, as your eyes have been licked clean of hope and fear. Here is the world as it has always been, always fresh.

Spaciousness overflowing, your hand reaching out to brush the sunshine into an empty cup, overwhelming, deeply moving, you are the fullness of emptiness.

Your eyes, life, the light, the spark, the illumination in as and through utter darkness.

Spinning in kaleidoscopic colors and sound, in the middle of the swirling an imaginary center appears. A phantom a ghost an empty gem, a moving pulsating jewel, most magnificent as it has no center, it is you.

Only in the reflecting the waves of apparent dissonance, the overtones, the undertones, the richness and lushness of this song, this key of wonder is struck and where the two apparent sides meet there is not even nothing.

The imaginary center explodes into everywhere and nowhere and suddenly you see the beauty, your unowned magnificence sparkling, and you cannot turn away as you are not separate from it.

Night lights to infinity, streetlights on the run. Daring dashing delightful, demanding you to play along. Every step is unfinished, every song is undone, every story collapses under the weight of your own love. You call out with longing, and you call out with joy, and you call out with tears, and you call out and you call out and you call out without fear…
There is no answer other than your very own heart song singing drifting desert sand dunes blowing silently along.

The rocks may feel uneasy on this path that leads nowhere, but when there's no one going… the softness in the air... colors streaming …awareness knowing not a step without this knowing that it is aware.

How impossibly gorgeous to try to dance to sing to describe the unknowable untouchable with words that only reference the pseudo reality created by these very words! Like trying to cut apart and piece together the sky, trying to sweep a rainbow into your heart, dust pans leak stars into sky, drunk on your own love that pours in and through you, emptying and filling itself simultaneously.

Swimming swirling around as in of and through the emptiness, wings unfurl, love flows. Aglow with wonder lighting up the heavens with reflections of your echoing love songs that sing you.
Wind twirls down the canyon and dances in the tree tops laughing and weeping amazed at its own amazement, delighting in its own delight, some of us are the songsters…

Self remains but is always known to be the dream. The beautiful temporary crystalline lens through which life is able to see touch and feel it's own aliveness.
We can only see through our point of view but it can be known and felt simultaneously that there are no reference points whatsoever.

The ribbon of thought between everything and nothing weaves tracery patterns of light and color and forms that seem to have a substantial separate existence. They seem to be reaching out to touch you to capture you to trace you into being, to hold the magic of existence in the palm of your hand.

Filigree notions raveling and unraveling, tattered fringes of what you believed to be true soar in the wind, and there is obviously no separation between wind and you and the soaring thought dream. Like a three dimensional template thrown over infinite color, patternless patterns, rhythmless rhythms dancing forming swirling dissolving grab you and dance you and twirl you into a timeline between birth and death.

The rain bled her eyes dry. They were empty of color of sound of shape of form. Kaleidoscopic fractals shimmered in her heart. Her desire her ache to taste the taste of that which she knew so deeply but could not capture or enunciate or deliberate or describe… and songs flung wide and here and there and closer and closer and closer touching kissing reaching deeply piercing her very heart your very heart our very heart. The very heart beat of existence, this as it is, twirling shining shimmering glimmering tracing itself into you and me. And love.

No longer looking to swallow the sky, the sky swallows you. As all words ideas concepts are learned shared, we are a patchwork quilt, made up, just like tomorrow and love. Life flows through us as us, here is our shared humanness, and yet everyone is a unique jewel. This flow of humanity though the ages is stunning! Everyone knows sorrow and joy and yearning and heartache and love and the pain of loss, and wonder. Such beautiful sorrow of the knowing of the precious tenuousness of this brief life. This is the wondrous ache that paints you into the picture.

There is no separation, no things or selves to be separate or joined. Knowing and feeling that deeply, always you are falling in love as love through love.

falling into the sunset
light breathing
reverberating into sound
wild eyed wonder
the measuring cup breaks
it all pours unhindered
light into light
a pure tone cannot be tied into knots
sublime edgeless-ness cannot be captured
pouring out pouring in leaking tears into this shoreless ocean
it fills your heart as you spill into it
seamless

Everyone knows the primordial ache of being alive, this longing, and some long to hear the song they sang as young children. The big wow that they believe they lost, a jewel they have been looking for their entire lives, yet the looking for it merely seems to create a distance between them and it that does not and has never existed. A trail of tears following you leading you compelling you to look to search to capture the magic that you are, captivated by your own beautiful sorrow, these tears that are yours, this love that you seek is yours, as you wander the desert dream your throat parched trying to dig in the sand to quench your thirst, exhausted, passing caravan after caravan stars streaming across the vastness the imaginary horizon always ahead.....
forever cutting the imaginary distance in half in half in half in half in

at midnight I lay back into the river of desire and the moon rose and erased the shadows of what I was supposed to be like, and how moonlight should dance, and I drowned in my own beautiful sorrow, this wondrous humanness, as my tears sang a eulogy to hope and fear
overtones of love reverberating without beginning or end revealed the crashing of forever and never as the shutters that seemed to conceal the light dissolved. no pictures were needed, no stopping no capturing no fixing this obvious beauty soaring glowing in me through me as me

We are the dance, spectacular beyond imagining, and yet we are imagined.

I catch a glimpse of myself in your eye, in your tears, in your showering love song. Mirrored reflections swimming flowing into and through themselves. Yet it is not me that I see and it is not you. It is not my heart that I feel nor is it yours. It is not my song that I sing, nor is it yours. It is dreams of love's memories flooding through me singing me. Collapsing submerging subsuming dissolved in memories. Imploding exploding... I can no longer find a counterpoint without your point. Without a ray a song a drop of dew a tear there is no reflection. We are unutterably magnificent in our shared humanness. A side long glance recognizing itself as it falls through the mirror that has no sides.

shine and shadow playing weaving intricate patternless patterns into a dance, shimmering rippling across uncharted bottomless depths where dreams held your fathomless beauty and wept softly echoing across the vastness, it was your own sobbing you heard late at night
she sang her name across the surface of the deep moon skimmed surface, and listened for a rippling echo of her heart song
and every note shimmered with her tears reflecting overtones of overwhelming wonder that caught her breath
a sudden unending hush a mad dance of expectancy for this for this for this for this

Truly truly there is just most wondrously this, there is no true self or true nature or God or anything lasting.
Nothing permanent nor impermanent.
Time is an illusion.
Self is an illusion.
Illusion is illusion.
All separate things or non things and separate moments, all events are illusion.
Yes there is life flowing, this aliveness you feel, no one or no thing makes it happen. It is not a whole bunch of inanimate goo somehow pierced by some intelligence or life force that animates it. It simply does itself.

You don't make life happen. I don't make life happen. God does not make life happen. There is no special core or kernel or special place that will last forever. No time nor non time. Nothing ever lasts… there are no things nor non things, there is no you or non you, there is no me there is no time nor non time, there is no place nor non place.

Ephemeral and dreamlike imaginary lines draw and erase them selves simultaneously. All separation is made up, this that is cannot be captured or divided in anyway, as there is nothing outside of it and there are no things inside of it. It is not an it, there are no its. There is no outside nor inside yet this includes all things.
We are nothing but a most marvelous brief shining transparent window through which life can see and touch and feel it's own aliveness. This magnificent dream of separation for no reason or non-reason allows life to touch itself. And in the touching we emerge.

There simply is no finger or no thing to be pointed at or nothing to be touched.
Can you pick up the moon's reflection in a pond, or does the attempt merely ripple the waters and reflect your beautiful hand your beautiful face your heart achingly beautiful humanness crying at the beauty of its own reflection?

Somehow it is realized that there is no separation, that it is all made up, a mental fabrication, that all the beliefs of who you were are like gossamer wisps of nothing, they unravel and dissolve. It was merely a tight knot of belief glued together with hope and fear.

You were merely a swirling of tattered remnants of thought and memory and learned shared words concepts ideas, beliefs in more and better in future in past, as the wind rips apart all ideas of love. Prayers falling into the hush of the night, not a word can alter the coming of dawn. When you recognize your heart song there is no doubt, you hear the beat it is your heartbeat, you sway to the music, you find you are the dancer and the dance, the singer and the song as it writes itself with filigreed patterns dissolving into and out of sea foam clouds streaming in the wind as the wind dissolves into itself…

A unique blend of learned shared words and concepts, memories swirling, a lens a prism creating infinite variety of things. In the twirling an imaginary center seems to emerge, and inside and outside and here and there and up and down, location, and time. A constant echo-location is required to find who and where you are on that imaginary timeline between birth and death.
When the story is known and felt to be simply a beautiful fairy tale, the constant angst and fear and feeling of effort of trying to create maintain and defend that imaginary character simply ends.

This is utterly intimate and raw, caring deeply yet impersonal, this unadorned unfettered life without anyone doing anything, and yet life still spontaneously does itself.
Once the story is no longer believed it becomes unowned and soon you become all stories.
Like infinite hands blooming, parentheses ricocheting reverberating endlessly inwards and outwards infinitely, feeling deeply all of the stories all of our beautiful humanness shared.
Infinite shades of tear stained cheeks and these very lips that sing and kiss the darkest night into light, life singing me singing you, explode into ever blooming ever receding wonderment. You fell through the looking glass enamored with your own reflection. Life kisses itself through this very echo that mirrors your beauty as it slides across the sea of dreams.

The first light of dawn waltzes through your mind stream and plays upon the ripples of light and shadow as the day time dream stretches your toes into the dance. When have you not been spinning with your shadow in an all embracing kiss? Your showering sparks of tears flung into cascades of color that light the universe with your beautiful reflection.
You are this kaleidoscopic watercolor dream casting shadows into shadows that ripple with an unhinged loveliness across this dreamscape that swallows you as you are dying of thirst, and leaves you abandoned, bereft of all ideas of tomorrow.

as you left looking for nothing and found the dream of everything sliding in you as you through you, of utter lushness and richness, emptiness ever blooming ever wilting…

It simply had never occurred to him that everything he knew was hearsay. That all of his thoughts were made of shared learned words. That the known world was simply a bunch of learned shared concepts, like a shimmering reflection, a castle built in mid air. It hit him like a bomb exploding inside into out, and outside into in, as he realized that all he could really know, but not in a conventional way, all he truly really was, was this un-interrupted indivisible symphony of perception and the simultaneous inseparable recognition of it. All ideas of knowing of capturing of understanding this edgeless center-less flowing simply fell away along with any idea of a separate know-er.

I yawn and rub my sleepy eyes, was it today that I remembered yesterday?
Waves never divide the ocean, and inchworms never measure the branch, and hours never split the day, and a flower cannot grow in space, and there is no separation in this wondrous dance that vividly appears as anything at all. fleeting evanescent ephemeral ambiguous a-temporal ungraspable magnificent…

Spiraling into infinity we dance in effortless union as we were never separate.
And it is sublime...
Utter spaciousness and no confinement, no bias, no center....
Nothing ever ever ever to hold onto...
No hands to hold…
Beauty bliss joy sorrow...
The surge of life defined...
Beauty stretches the edges of the mind and color leaks out, pooling in delicious unknown flavors where we dance in love's embrace.
Without you there is no one to lose themselves in the butterfly's last flight before dusk, or feel the softness without touching.
No longer chasing the ever receding horizon wind blows through us and we are the wind.

Our sails unfurled and broke away from the ship and carried us with wings of love into magical dimensionless space.
No longer trying to count the waves on the ocean there is no one to be free...
This precious momentary is a jeweled ship on an ocean of jewels leading nowhere
The heart drops, and we are smitten with the fleeting essence of this.
Ripples in the wind blow softly across your tender skin.
Sorrow, joy, unwound the center-less center.
There's a beauty in the lost ness, the feeling of a barely remembered melody.
Tears, the wetness singing salty dreams of what can never be known. So easily we slide into our softness, the unfindable spaces between us, rhythm less patterns speaking in tongues.
Tears the language of love

we exist like a phantom
between the words and the song
and how many poems laugh and sing and fall away
before the texts are unopened
the stars fall out of your eyes and write ancient words of longing on the tip of your tongue
that linger
and dance in the moonlight
cricket song

She was her dress of love and sorrow woven with tales of moonlight playing on the garden path.
Love is a daydream, as real as tomorrow
Only in our brokenness, when we realize even love is made up, is there the recognition of the utter emptiness of all thingness, including the recognizer. There was never anyone to be broken.
Twisting twining never capturing anything words create beautiful visual deeply felt patterns that stir light into the dream. Shimmering sourceless reflections echo and sing you and me and we and love.
It's like the sun finally rises above the high canyon walls and the warmth greets the light that's been here for hours...

We all know the feeling of love, and that the word is a paltry pointer to the hugeness of the feeling. The word wind does not blow, it does not even move, or dance or swing. The word fire does not burn, it's not even hot. The word tears is not wet, nor salty.
Have you ever watched the sky as day turns into night? There is no place no time, no dividing line. The word mountain doesn't put a line around a mountain and separate it from a valley. There is no mountain that can be contained. They are all different. Some have rocky cliffs, deep clear lakes, multiple peaks, meadows, clearings in the summer that are filled with a riot of flowers and insects buzzing and deer, pausing, little cabins with smoke curling out the chimney...
Mountain is just a word a concept that paints an image, and allows your brain to 'know' it. It seems like you can draw a line around it, but what do you do when you get to the bottom? where does the mountain end and the valley begin?
There really are no separate things or events. There is no beginning nor end to a moment, and no you separate and apart from from what's going on to capture a moment, or life.

Words seem to create a universe of separate things, like billiard balls hitting each other. What's going on is edgeless and fluid and cannot be caught or captured with words.
Yet this pseudo reality painted by the thought stream, this conceptual reality this magician's tale, is the only place where you and I and love and beauty exist. It's wondrous what the mind creates. This flowing water color dreamscape of this and that is painful when separation is believed.
As soon as I speak, here I am, here we are. Lets meet at that little cabin on the edge of the cliff and watch the sun set.
listen to the mountain
watch day turn into night
and fall in love…

Words arise and seem to separate what cannot be caught or named or split apart, and some reflect an echo of seamlessness. Swirling and tumbling, resplendent with awe that sparkles in its own reflection. This silence sings itself as memories appear and fall through themselves like mist dissolving into this intricate jeweled

218

tapestry. Constantly unwoven as the tattered threads reunite and create the fabric anew without beginning or end. It always beginning and always ending. Such obvious pulsating aliveness reaching out to kiss itself through your beautiful beautiful eyes.

This deep current of emotion like a sparkling river needs its banks to flow.
Sometimes the river looks around and gazes upon its own beauty and weeps.
Wet in wet in wet...
I am these tears reflecting ripples of light flowing into and through each other painting this sonorous rush of life that fills me and empties me.
Empty winds skim the surface, iridescence smiles, and I recognize my face, lost in wetness, in love with its own shimmering.
You can feel the pull towards the shoreless sea which you have never left. Inevitably you drown in your own wonder and delight of the taste of taste, like love drops merging coalescing falling through the imaginary spaces illuminated from within. Whirlpools of pure space singing. Playfully joyfully, awe unwraps wonder and and stirs itself into the dance of you and me and we.

music seems to go this way and that, but the melody is never lost or found, the dance floor drops away yet the dance remains… a fiery dance ....intertwined.... enveloped ...held ...in nothing as nothing, resembling everything…
its the swirling, light and life and wind soaring through you as you, infinite colors and hues sweep you into the dance, utterly astonished that this unknowable dancing dances itself, no steps are found, no footprints are left upon the mantel, there was no door nor anyone to leave or enter…

.....and bursting endlessly in timeless beauty, I slide effortlessly through this sea of delight and there is no need to capture rhyme or reason in this endless unstoppable surge of intoxicating awe. I am a story of wind soaring through itself and disappearing into its own brushstroke, I slide effortlessly through this sea of delight with liquid eyes. Myriad rainbow hues effortlessly spinning outward and in through unspeakably vast untraceable space echoing in the stars and heard again in every drop of midnight.

All I know is that I don't know anything. And that there is no one to know or not know...
And the recognition of the fleeting ambiguous nature of reality is the most magnificent recognition. Ever.
And to know that we know this is even more marvelous more supreme than every dream coming true forever…

The tempest that slew you was your own love and desire. The prism that seems to separate light into infinite colors is you! Clear transparent radiance sings vibrates breathes a hush a sigh a silent sonic boom that shatters all ideas of who you are
Who you were
And who you should or could be
It's like time dies
All lines written with invisible ink
Never caught one breath
Not one parcel of time
Nor one bit of up
was grasped
You look and you look and you look and you look, and you cannot find one thing to hold onto. You search the vastness and cannot find anyone who could hold. You dissolve in your tears as you fall into vastness, utter spaciousness blooming, exploding, your heart is utterly naked as the universe flows through you, as you flow through the universe.

Constantly writing itself, jumping into the unknown, like a cloud caressing sky as it falls through its own caress.
A lifetime of tension that had pressed the earth and sea against sky exploded into infinite tears. All boundaries collapsed in a tsunami of unutterable dimension and a seamless shimmering reflected my unknown face from everywhere and nowhere.
Inside and outside were no more as future and past slipped into the vastness.. I could not turn away from my own unbearable beauty, the universe painting itself with reflections of sky.

I was stunned. the person I had thought I was was simply a knot of beliefs and preferences yet underneath them there was absolutely nothing. The ropes that had held a great balloon tied to the ground had become unraveled, and there was now an incredible spaciousness. All belief was seen as fiction, a character in a movie. I could find only a sublime emptiness where those beliefs had been, and it was a fluidity filled with whatever seemed to be going on at the time, nothing constant, nothing to hold onto, no control, even this character appearing, disappearing, always an endless slipping into emptiness.

walking in wonder, stardust glimmers in my forgotten footsteps creating shadows of nothingness from imaginary tales, and the moon seems more luminous in my skirt of dancing shadows as ripples of starlight cascade through the illusory space where love flows.
I need a space suit and gossamer wings to play in the dream, this rainbow cloak seems to create this character of a dancing girl. Echoes stream through me as my hair blows from side to side. This starlit blanket wraps around me and I am starlight itself. Lost forever as emptiness and found again in the storybook of love.

And the edgeless-ness pulls you in.
And you are lost forever.
And it is sublime magic.
You look around and lose yourself in the beauty, and it is completely beyond anything you ever imagined.
And all description slips into nothingness, you are beyond any need to capture.
It is ultimate spaciousness
supreme... vastness...awe...
I blink my eyes and the miracle is still here...
My very breath blows me away
All ordinariness is gone
There is nothing that is not spectacular.
There are no things…

There is a profound shift.. It is not a one time experience. Life is lived fully, there is a sense that everything that is going on is a

miracle and a calm abiding knowing that labels and words do not actually divide this world, that there is no division or split felt anywhere, all description is meaningless, all sense of lack vanishes, there is no hope or fear or need of a never arising next. She could no longer turn away from the beauty as it was everywhere and nowhere.
Darkness danced inside her shadow, illumined with sparks of her reflection.
There was no then or other
No more or less
And no now
Flickering three D ancient movies spilling her tale upon the screen
As she watched the memory of her shadow dance behind it.

Following a gesture towards the door she turned around and not even an outline of a kiss was left in the footlights. This is indeed a magnificent dream, a magician's tale told by no one.
Infinite filigreed lines form and erase them selves
Creating a crescendo a music box
Of lives in anticipation
A wave surging and mounting and aching for release
Of a silent walled in you
Your empty pockets filled with dreams of tomorrow
Of a day when the sun will rise and never set
When you will be held and never let go
When you will be one with everything and everyone
And become selfless and desire-less
And compassionate and loving
And peaceful
And enlightened…

Looking for life for meaning in a book
Trying to peer in between the words
Dying of thirst
Desperately hoping to drink the word water
The net of words can never capture water
No matter how many time it's thrown
Sometimes the tears flow so that you slip down the banks of the stream and drown.

You realize that all thingness is mentally fabricated by thought
words ideas concepts
Made up
Just like you
You discover you can breathe underwater
Suspended as nothingness, neither ok nor not ok
The fullness rushed back in all at once
I wept and wept
Here I was
Much like before.....
And I saw that self was desire
The ache of our beautiful shared humanness
The greatest peace is knowing we are each other
The end of self judgement and self correction.
The end of trying to fix the self or others or the world
A seamless flow without cause and effect

within the symphony of perception there is an undeniable silence
singing
within the dance of time there is a stillness
moving
words seem to create a wall between a you
and what is going on
trying to erase your timeline creates it
trying to peer beneath the words
writes them
under your beautiful garment of utter nakedness
There is not even nothing
you have never been separate
you are this center-less radiant indivisible jewel
slow dancing in wild magnificence
Even meaninglessness loses its grasp.
The primordial hum of your own aliveness always on, always
magnificent is only recognized through this web of imaginary
thingness. This cats cradle never caught a piece of sky. Yet sky
and all and everything is magnificent beyond measure. Unbearably
beautiful
Wordless wonder sings.
As we dissolve into each others shadows
Overlapping like midnight ocean…

Self, an imaginary character, does not wake up, or the ego die. It's realized that you and all thingness is made up and that's that. It is all a mental fabrication, there is no escape, anything the mind can come up with, all description, is more dream stuff, including this. Even edgeless seamless center-less vastness is description. There are no reasons or non reasons, life simply happens, of itself so. There is nothing outside of it, and no things inside of it. What is going on has no name nor non name, it has no edges or center, it cannot be caught with the razors of words or concepts. It is simply beyond belief or understanding or imagination or description yet includes all these things.

it is not zero or one or two or three, it is not measurable nor non measurable, there is no purpose nor non purpose. The physical world exists yet it has no qualities or characteristics, no time dimension or causality no measurement no this or that without the objectifying human brain. The intellectual understanding may precede the shift in perception yet it is not necessary, as enlightenment, like all of like simply cannot be understood. There is no outside nor anyone to step there to capture it or understand it.

caressed and kissed from the inside and out, there is no place, not even placeless-ness, that is not your embrace
softness falling though softness into itself
and my words like the prow of a ship never divide the sea yet ripples form and the waves crash into themselves and clothe the dream with a shimmering iridescence made of echoes and reflections of their own reflections
there is no singer when there is no song
how beautifully life breaks our hearts, this joy and the sorrow that we can feel so much, so deeply
how wondrous this life this brief brief tenuous song sung for no one by no one
how we knew it was magic, how we tried to catch it to keep it to hold it in the palm of our hands, to treasure it in our hearts created an imaginary distance between us and it
never suspecting that we were the magic the jewel the shimmering the love that we longed for

you reach a point where you have read all you can read where every hand you've held starts to dissolve and every bright promise of a future starts to fade. you begin to fall into this sinking feeling that there's nothing else than this… ever gasping for breath you turn around thinking maybe you could go back to another time when you believed all the lies but there's nothing there, you can't find your shadow or your footsteps

All I had tried to run away from circled around and kissed me full on the mouth.
More intimate than this very breath, closer than thought or feeling or even love.
It slaughtered me and I found myself again resting in my own beautiful embrace weeping
I am this beautiful heartache.

The pages unravel themselves as the story is told, and a beautiful sublime bittersweet melancholy echoes in infinite ripples through your empty footsteps.
Golden coins toss themselves into the ripples, flowers bloom and wilt, suspended as the sea of dreams, joy sorrow longing love awe …wordlessly I sing.
Truly the un-catchability, the impermanence I feared became life's beauty. Knowing that this is indeed it and there is no next, there is sublime ease.
The rest I always sought was always here saturating the dream.
Words reference other words concepts other concepts ideas other ideas. Looking for the meaning of life in a dictionary will leave you drowning in a bowl of alphabet soup.
How many decades did I try peer underneath the words, look between the lines and squiggles to try to catch the magic of what I knew was right here on the tip of my tongue! Yes, it is on the tip of your tongue, but it can never ever be uttered, as life cannot be captured, it is not a thing, and there is no you separate from it to catch it. There are no things.
What is there between the breath and the song?
What is not a what?
Trying to capture what is going on, trying to put together what was never separate into a place of rest or understanding most painfully perpetuates the illusion that there is someone separate from what's

going on. Yet as long as you feel separate you are defined by this effort

Have you ever found an edge or outside to what is going on?

Is there an outside to what is going on?

...or are there no sides?

If there are no sides or non-sides is there a middle?

You cannot step outside of what seems to appear and manipulate it or accept it or reject it or surrender to it.

There is no it nor you.

Your Own Love Calls You Home

River kisses itself through your lips
Night drinks day
Life swallows you
As you tip this empty glass
Marveling at your own reflection
Swirling down the river
Scintillating aliveness
Breathes wind
Breathes you
Breathes the waves that capsized the ocean
Where the sun and moon drowned

Where is everything?
Where is nothing?
Where is the place where love and emptiness kiss?
Where is the shine?
Where is the shadow?
Where is the place where long green grasses wave over your
grave

Who took an empty breath when there was no one breathing
No one weeping
No one singing

sunset fills your skies
death's brush colors
your aliveness with
unbearable preciousness

sailing nowhere
yet there is wind

this scintillating aliveness shines
rippling wet through wetness
heartbeat of this and that sings

no safe harbor where you can hide
no map or sextant
yet stars
and moon and sun
slide across the vastness

looking for a new day
seems to obscure the sun
that is shining
that is setting
I see your tender beauty reflecting
in your eyes

I can never kiss this all encompassing love, yet somehow it kisses
me

It is far grander than love or beauty or awe itself
It is life kissing itself through you
And knowing it

Morning fills the canyon with light and bird song
Piercing my eyes
My ears
My heart

No one is asleep
No one awakens
There is simply this
What seems to appear
It can feel seamless
Or not
All perception arises equally and evenly and is simultaneously
inseparably recognized evenly and equally without any effort
without anything needing to be done

The longing for tomorrow leaves on the dream train called time

This is our only home, this dream of dancing shadows. Can you see your reflection on the canyon wall, sliding along with the moonscape, rushing toward the sea?

Can you see how every shared learned word paints the dreamscape into separate things and events? Even these words as you read them seem to paint a morning and a separate you.

But morning and the sound of the tea kettle are not separate, nor the light pouring through the window. You'd have to capture life and put it into buckets to make it separate from you. You cannot be separate from the attempt to capture it, this longing for solidity, this fear of unknowing, this fear of emptiness,
this fear of death.

The terrifying beauty of life's fluidity is not a stranger to you, yet it creates a painful dissonance with the belief in solidity, the belief in other better more and next.

What we feared the most
The nakedness
To feel all this love we were afraid to lose
This impermanence
Is the beauty
...we are this fleeting flowing beauty.

Without beginning or ending this fairytale that blooms and wilts simultaneously is this very unspeakable unbound lush rich beauty. I am simply a storybook character who seemed to lose her way as the pages fell apart and flew away with the wind. Singing soaring sky and blue into existence where memories no longer gather by the sea longing for the big wow. It only seemed that there was a someone and a place to land. It only seemed like she had lost this heart magic...

It seems I am always weeping... tho you may not see my tears

They have no time or name
Joy sorrow love... nothing at all but this beauteous feeling of
seamlessness... of edges seeming to appear yet feeling sublime
edgleless-ness...
Colors appear and swirl into wildflowers by the trail as my shadow
precedes me... I fall in love with everyone I see... with thingness
itself strewn across the vast unknown...

This is as real as it gets...
This is it coyote...
....knowing that all separation is made up, is not the end of the
conceptual world, the only world we exist in, the only world we can
know... of you and me and this and that.

How cruel to deny someones death... and the pain a widow feels,
yet I have seen that happen in some non-duality circles.

When no separation is realized you don't go around saying, 'I don't
exist!'. You feel deeply the pain of everyone, as there is no
separation. it is intensely beautiful, immensely intimate, the awe
permeates all and everything. Simultaneously surreal and real-er
than real, raw, naked, life full on, unadorned. I never speak about
this to people I know in person, unless someone asks. I am
surrounded by seekers and they are beautiful just as they are.

I would say that you fall and fall and fall (actually it is like crashing
though a million mirrors, with every shard piercing your heart), until
the falling is falling, and there is no one left to fall..., no handholds
are left, no reference points whatsoever. I remember one of my
favorite lines of Alan Watts for decades was, (approximately),
'Indeed, you were thrown off a cliff the day you were born, and
there is no use clinging to the rocks that are falling with you'. I used
to read his book, 'The Wisdom of Insecurity' just to feel like my
hands were off the handlebars, if only for a moment. It felt so
wondrous, and I had no idea how it would hurt so much to have this
become the case. (this seamlessness always was, yet it was simply
not recognized).

Edgeless river
Neither moving nor non moving
Flows
And me, an apparent whirl-pooling of wet in wet, can only know the stream of perception and its inseparable recognition from this apparent point of view, feeling that there are no separate points. Feeling that there are no things permanent or unchanging. No thing that I am, yet, no thing that I am not. No things nor non things, yet all and everything seem to arise and self release without time or non time in this edgeless streaming momentary that burns itself in this seamless immediacy.

Falling in love as love through love…
Constantly self arising and simultaneously self releasing, this life this life this life this life, this magnificent aliveness that I can never know how or why, or capture, and not feeling separate from it, I no longer care to.

Always knowing deep down that life is magical you feared its end. Trying to capture that magic made you feel separate from it. But it's not an it, it has no sides, there is no outside to life, can you find an edge to what's going on? Can you find a before or next?

Where are the characters in last night's dream?
Where is yesterday's sunset?
Where is the dawn of tomorrow?

This is it coyote.

There is no day nor morning when you will awaken. There is no more or less than this, wherever seems to appear, whatever it looks or feels like. You know this yet it is frightening!
What would you do if there were no next?
What could you do?
What would you add or take away from what's going on?
If there is no outside how could you?
Where would it go?
If there's no outside that you can find, how could you possibly step outside of this seamless edgeless flow and change it or accept it or reject it or surrender to it?

You are not separate from this symphony of perception and its inseparable recognition.
If you feel separate, do you feel separate from the feeling of separation?
No escape, is there???

Looking for solidity, for permanence, as well as looking for enlightenment, keeps the illusion of a prize and someone to get it.
Keeps the feeling of distance
Of better
Of next
Alive.

How deep the shadow sliding down the sidewalk?
How far or near this intimate feeling of sun dancing on your cheek?
How close this sensation of wind?
How far light...

How shallow or deep is time as you slide along with your shadow, inseparable from this ever emerging, ever dissolving sound and light show?
How wide the day?
How narrow the night...
How precious this aliveness
That cannot be caught
Yet is always known
Inseparable from the symphony of perception and its inseparable recognition.
Ease-fully and naturally life simply happens.
All by itself.
Without effort or non effort
Wind
Sun
Light
Shadow

How deep is this touch-less touch when we fall into and through each others reflection?
How wondrous wonder

How magical love
Nothing can be grasped
There is no one to catch the wind who is separate from it.
No one separate from thought, feeling, sensation to choose it or alter it.
No one separate from life to hold it.
No one separate from this magical aliveness to understand or grasp it.

There are no separate moments
There is no time when you will awaken.
No past no future
No now.

I remember when the parameters of who I thought I was began to fall away. Such an immense feeling of freedom! At first they were ideas that I didn't like about myself, yet soon I realized, like a punch in the gut, that the ideas about myself that I liked would have to go as well.

As I began to feel free-er and free-er, it seemed like the goal, so to speak would be to feel free of my 'afflictive' feeling and thought, and be washed away into nothingness.

I fell and fell and fell until there was no one to fall, no where to land, no one to land, no reference points whatsoever...

I was suspended as nothingness, and it was nothing to sing about. When the fullness rushed in that summer afternoon, I wept.

...and wept and wept and wept... here were all the feelings I was trying to get rid of, full on, this nakedness that no one wore was inseparable from feeling....

No feelings are owned, I get to feel it all, the world weeps through me.

There is no line or shadow between you and the world... all is self illumined, from within from without from everywhere, from nowhere, there are no directions, no paths, no signs in this present called life, called now, which has no name nor non name as it has no edges or center. Just an imaginary center that seems to know that it is imaginary.

Knowing and feeling that here and there and this and that is made up, yet here we are, naked unadorned dancers in this pirouette of life, this ballet this tango this monster mash, this pas-de-deux, this one-step, this two-step, this call and answer love song ricocheting through the canyon of love.

The longing to capture the magic of wind...
Is recognizing of the beauty of impermanence.
If you truly knew this
There would be the feeling that you are the wind
As wind, as life, flows through you...

For what would you do with it
The wind
The magic of life
That flows all by itself
Where would you put it
If you could?

Are you separate from this flowing?
Is there an outside
Is there an inside....

The razor of thought cannot know or capture this edgeless seamless-ness.

But you can feel it deeply
You always have

You are not separate from this feeling.

and when all ideas dry up of what life should or could be like
looking for a method or a way to live
there is simply life doing itself
unspeakably beautiful

Unashamedly naked
No hope for the clothes of dawn
Nor fear of night

Falling in love with the fluidity of this aliveness,
falling in love with falling in love with falling in love with falling in
love....

There is no actual color outside your brain
Just wavelengths of varying degree
How marvelous we perceive brightly colored objects
The brains of some birds and butterflies seem to be responding to
wavelengths our brains apparently do not respond to
Yet we can never know what the world or color looks like to them
...Or our closest lover

Why would you want to get rid of self? To be free of 'afflictive'
thought and feeling? Obviously if there were a thinker or feeler or
someone separate from these, that imaginary chooser would be
choosing nice happy fluffy emotion and easeful thought, yes?

There really is no outside to this stream of perception and its
inseparable recognition, so it's not really an it, is it? Can you grab
something and remove it from all this? Where would it go? Can you
add something? Where would it come from? Can you step outside
of all this and manipulate or accept or reject or surrender to it?

Self doesn't go away. It's merely seen and felt that there is no
solidity, nothing permanent, essentially empty... simply perception,
thought sensation feeling flowing, without the feeling that there is a
thinker feeler doer.

Still there are deep deep feelings
Sorrow joy ...the sweetness of being able to feel so fully, unafraid,
without hope or fear of a never arising next.

The entire symphony of perception and its inseparable recognition
is all a complete confirmation of your beautiful aliveness.

Life happening all by itself, all of a piece, of itself so.

Can you see that NOTHING you've ever tried to do or not do has ever brought you permanent relief? Perhaps not one step closer to this elusive goal? Perhaps there is no escaping your beautiful humanness. Perhaps this is it coyote. Perhaps there REALLY is no next.

The citadel of the assumption of knowing and the fear of not must be constantly repaired lest the light shine through...

No one really knows what will happen, or if there will be a next. Life happens all by itself, you've never done a thing.

No one really even knows what's going on apart from the symphony of perception and the simultaneous inseparable recognition of it. We assume the physical world exists.

We can never know what it's like for another
We are all truly alone
But
We can be alone together

Some appear to know that there is no next, that this is indeed it, others seem to live in a state of constant hope and fear of a never arising next, no one chooses how to feel. There is no right or wrong way to feel, simply feeling, thought, sensation happening.

There is such a terror of letting go.... which leaves when there is the recognition that there is no one to let go... that there truly are no separate things to grasp...

And life feels like it's flowing through you as you. Life with no one at the helm is intensely full on...

This step-less path to no where is lined with tears
They are no one's but uniquely yours

Awakening is quite simply unimaginable. Even those who have had a glimpse of this cannot conjure up this indubitable knowing feeling of sublime seamlessness. It is beyond belief or understanding and that is why some question me when I sing about enlightenment. Here there is no doubt and no place for it to arise that this is the profound shift in perspective that sages have been singing about through out time. To some it may seem that this certitude is hubris, but I'm not trying to convince anyone of anything. Some of us are simply the songsters. Life flows through me as me and sings a love song that may echo your heart song.

If you feel like you have had a glimpse of this, or that you got it somehow and then you somehow lost it, you never really did have this as no one gets this. How can you become what you already are, how can you capture what already is, how you can you slide into your own footprints?

For when you look, what is going on is far too simple and far too complex and fluid to capture isn't it? It's quite obvious that there is no edge or outside, or beginning or end to what is going on. Attention may seem to wander and then rest, wander and then rest, as the thought stream describes it, seemingly stopping and isolating separate things and moments. But it's apparent that there is much much more that these words are not seemingly capturing. There also may be memories, and thought dreams of the future, regrets and hopes and fears slip sliding along, in this bare back ride of what you call your life.
It never stops does it? This symphony of perception and of thought, this aliveness recognizing itself instantaneously spontaneously in the ever emerging immediacy.
You have never been apart from life, nor the thought stream, nor the flow of perception. Truly, unless thought tries to think about thought, or change it, there doesn't seem to be a hiccup.

Life is far too vast, infinite beyond measure, to escape or capture or know, and also naturally intimate as you are always here. So perhaps you are also un-capture-able and fluid and unknowable. What are the limits that seem to define you without thought? Where are any edges without thought?

What would you be without the definition of 'I once had this, but now I've lost it'? What would you be without this longing to get it back? What if you are this longing? What if you are this longing to escape the confines of longing? What if this is indeed it, including this longing that you are?
What if there is no next, no future, when you will get this?

I wandered through a garden of sunflowers swirling in goldfinches, and ponds of sparkling song, looking for the other side of love. The kiss of a beggar hungering for her own lips, drinking silent sorrow. It was there in the softness of yellow, it was there in the swooping of wings. It was there as I gazed at my reflection on the muddy banks where cottonwoods thrust their thirsty dragon feet into the wetness and stretched their arms and feathered hands into sunlight. It was never lost, this bursting heart, it only seemed to fade as I learned the names of color.
Looking for winged moon glow, soaring as this sparkling river of memory, as infinite facets of yesterday.
Doves hover by the feeder, one crashes into my window and leaves her feathered glance on the glass. She flies away into the garden and her magic of flight alights on my lips, for it is this kiss I have always been, the desire to dance, this song of life, as it sings me.

This unutterable vacancy of even emptiness and vastness, and the mind shattering melancholic beauty of your ultimate aloneness slides through the mirror and into itself. The taste of this life without edges where sorrow and joy and love swirled into a heart ache that escaped the imaginary confines of an owner, of a home whose windows were broken long ago. The looking out kissed the looking in, the mirror was found to have no sides, nor middle.
Transparent crystalline endless blue fell through the ceiling as earth and sea crashed into sky. Blue into blue into blue into blue, and blue became meaningless.
Mind conjures infinite mirrored facets inscribing the dream with unending wonder and unspeakable beauty. Coalescing as this flowing thought dream singing a story where the center has dropped out.

First fallen leaves of autumn, scattered golden flowers blooming upon the path, nestling into the drifting feathers of wind shredded bark. Two children marvel at an ant carrying a bit of leaf and the mother marvels with them. I tell her she is beautiful. She smiles, and I catch a glimpse of my own radiance. Hot tears drying on my face, oh yes, here I am, waking along talking along singing these love songs with you. Love flows in this canyon of imaginary separation and paints our delicate tender outlines with this unspeakable flood of life kissing itself in a never ending always ending precious kiss.

An unfathomable love of love's beauty sweeps through me in this always obvious swoon. Just as it seems to appear, feet padding down the trail, storm clouds blossoming, taking pictures for passersby, feeling deeply the pain of a lover, longing to soothe another's belief in the dream, knowing all I can do is love them, my skirt softly caressing my ankles, an unexplained tiredness, a jay song sings with the traffic, wind begins to ripple the late summer golden grasses into a pirouette as I wonder if I have a plastic bag for my phone for the coming rain, a soundlessness within sound, a seamless hush within the silence, a raw unadorned life of knowing this is it, always, sings through these very lips that no longer hunger for a tomorrow.

Utterly satiated with this desire to sing.

Words can never catch this splendid beauty, yet beauty is a word. There are no love songs that will ever caress you as I long to, yet I sing. This life this life this life, un contained unfettered, beyond all ideas of freedom, all ideas of love, wondrous beyond belief or imagination flowing freely through me in me as me. Impossible to escape the dream but knowing it is a dream, and longing to sing of it, knowing this wordless song cannot be sung.

You waltzed into the sun's gaze alive fire blazing, lost, transfixed with unutterable beauty. This is knowing and feeling you are and all things are simply fleeting description. Even the knowing feeling that there never was a home nor you to leave it is the dream weaving and unweaving itself. Even these words as my thumb pats them on the screen is the dream painting itself. Only in this dance, in the Grand Canyon of love, is there beauty. It simply feels like there's nothing here, yet I am always rapt in my infinite intimate embrace. Joy love comfort love desire awe, familiar and new, this sparkling ache for what is, taps you on the shoulder and you whirl around and catch a glimpse of your beauty and emptiness as it flows through you as you. Everywhere and nowhere is home yet there is no home... extending infinitely outward and inward in every direction with no direction or time filling you emptying you. A sliding love poem singing itself kissing itself through your lips your song your edgeless heart.

Deep within the desert I lost my meandering footprints trying to lose my alone-ness, my lostness that was always on the tip of my tongue.
I poured a thousand sorrows into a China cup and placed it on the window sill, and left it for the moon to swallow.. Diaphanous dragon clouds drank its iridescence and my tears traced delicate shades of unknowing into this paper heart that kept folding into itself as it was ripped apart by the recognition of my ultimate emptiness. I could not take refuge under the oak tree that stretched out its limbs to gather sunlight, as it was grown in sky. All cloud castles crumbled, the scaffolding of hope that held up my world toppled. Dreams of another step were filled with a heaviness, and a sweet ache that was swallowed by the very earth this very song that blossoms into this color this sound this very light of darkness, this weight of light that swoons into itself within the racing river of my heart. No longer mine, this origami heart that was simply made of Imaginary lines drawn around a shimmering river of echoed vastness unfolded. All ideas of love flew away with tomorrow.
Shadows dance on the sidewalk.
Midnight flowers bloom, night air sparkles and awe abounds.
Love swoons into itself.

Love flows in this canyon of imaginary separation and paints our delicate tender outlines with this unspeakable flood of life kissing itself in a never ending always ending precious kiss. This life this life this life, un contained unfettered, beyond all ideas of freedom…

I remember when the beliefs that there was a right or wrong way to eat to act to feel to think to love to live to die formed my imaginary lines.

Such freedom beyond freedom when all beliefs are seen through! How marvelously unbelievable when it's realized there is not even nothing under the cloak of beliefs! The glue of hope and fear has dissolved and light pours through you as you. Light weaving and unweaving itself into a flowing dream gown of glowing awe.

...and when did the sun plan to shine upon your tears
...and the wind to dry them?
When did the moon plan to pull your heart into the sky?
Broken necklaces in the sand like scattered love letters, jewels flung across the universe, your eyes are starlight dancing.
Translucent tears color infinity. It's all a flowing self portrait. There are no things to understand as this vast vacancy is empty of even emptiness. It's this beautiful unknowing that you fear that defines you, as you sense it will be the end of you.
You may run down main street into the forest fleeing your utter nakedness, but your love will find you and expose every secret corner of your being until there is no where left to hide. Until there's no where to run, and no one to run.
Life is slippery when it's realized that life has no edges, nor do you. A most wondrous feeling of lostness can occur and an intuited knowing that this knowing can't be captured.

I emerge from the flowing casting stones across the waters delighting in watching the rippling reflections. Amazed at my own amazement, merging again into the seamless river. The home I never left. There was no one to leave or arrive.

Cricket song smooths the edges where you tried to scratch a hole into the sky. Where your heart lay bleeding into the sunset, past and gone, where is this gash, apart from wonder?
Where is this love, apart from you?
Where is anything where is nothing?
The love the silence the cacophony of traffic, softly padding feet on shadowed sidewalk, sliding into the patterns that are only glimpsed

out of the corner of your eye ...memories have lost their grip and I cannot find them. A few swirl around to remind me of who I was, walking in moonlight streetlight midnight.

Wind is a word, yet it points to seamless beauty cast by imaginary lines. Simultaneously arising and disappearing, yet recognized. Some realize the seeing is not separate from the see-er or the seen. All three just clumsy ways of describing the same unutterable unknowable. Life paints and erases itself.

I held moonlight in the palm of my hand ....and saw my own face in the wonder.

The only world you can ever know is this, just as you think it is, just as you think you are. You are an imaginary reference point around which the dream of this and that swirls, spinning though your synapses. The thought stream paints this and that. Outside of the spinning there is not even nothing. There is no outside. There is no escape. This is it, coyote. Those who are trying to stop thought believing it is the culprit for their pain do not realize that without thought they are not. It is not thought that is the cause of the problem, it is belief in it which creates the desire to escape. The umbrella you held so bravely in the dark never could protect you from drowning in your tears, or the love you feared to feel so deeply as you knew it would wash you away.

Under the umbrella of words we splash in our own wetness, super saturated with the love of all and everything knowing there are no things, nor an outside to this amazing embrace of our own loving arms. Love dances nakedly, awash in love with itself, seen only through the tender delicate wetness of our eyes. Full on unadorned life floods through us as us, and we discover our feet have always known this dance.

...you scan all the tears you've shed for the ultimate words, but you cannot find this placeless-ness where you might be free...
...you feel there must be a key to unlock the treasure chest of your heart, of what you know has been lost... you find yourself lost at sea... every path has led nowhere ...the storm you've longed for

242

and dreaded hits... you are struck by the golden sunset that captured your dreams... your flimsy raft of beliefs lashed together with hope and fear collapses and you drown in the depths where hidden rainbows swim... and moonlight glints like silver fish within the sea of nothing... and in this watery home you find you can breathe.. and no longer trying to escape, you're home.
You had never left.

Wind rises and ripples spill your heart to every unseen shore, and you no longer try to hold a part of it, for the fear of losing what never was spilled itself through you long ago. Unstained, the wine washed out and the intoxication never left.
All the ghosts and goblins, all that you feared arrived unbidden, and swept you away with the tides of unknowing.

You entered the dragons lair and were chewed up and spit out, and all the sparkling jewels were always reflecting your own brilliance, every nuance and hue, every song and footstep, every inseparable moment exploding imploding, yet never seen when you tried to see it.

Rudderless ghost ships meeting in the hush between the breath and the song.
Always simply just this as it is. All you ever thought you wanted sank to the bottomless bottom with your heart, and you rise through through the bubbles... surface into your own reflection, and look around. The wet has no beginning and no end. There is a tenderness in this for all and everyone for everything. A luminous diaphanous light gown woven with tears.
After the shift the story still writes itself but it's like it is never read. No bookmarks placed. No longing to peek to the last page or rewrite the first. There is no one to pay attention to it anymore. No one to say, 'oh I should've done this', or 'oh my I must do this next'. No more trying to fix the story or predict the middle or ending. The ever emerging edgeless momentary burns itself out as soon as it appears. Like a shooting star we are the light emerging and simultaneously disappearing. There is no one gripping and no things left to grip.

The sea sings, you are it's echo, you are drunk on your love. It has sunk you and drowned you, and bled you, fed you to the ends of a shore that could never be found or lost in your heart.
Skinless we soar, footless we dance.
Emptiness overflows.

He spent a lifetime trying to find the taste of taste. The meaning of meaning. Peering through the lines and squiggles of words, just knowing there was a treasure underneath, using more and more words to try to find their meaning their essence. He could never grasp life. All trying simply seemed to tie his heart in more knots, and block the light. He finally realized that the word water was not wet, nor the word salty, salty. The word tears did not feel hot and wet nor slide down his cheeks.
It's not that the word was not the thing. There were no things. It was only words that formed the imaginary lines around mountains and valleys and clouds. And him.

It is your love that sneaks up on you and slays you. You thought it was the night hawk on the mountain, or the sun rising over the rippling prairie… wings outstretched... soaring... beyond here and there... where edges crashed into the sea falling off an imaginary horizon.

On her mantle sing rainbow winds that cool her brow and tear her eyes. Her heart knows the backbeat to every song sung and unsung. Figures of emptiness blew away in the night and left echoes of shells and pieces of tattered paper whose words no longer called out to be read. She was the tree tops dancing in the wind and waves of grasses flowing in the canyon and the slow dance of cottonwoods in the moonlight. Starlight kissing her naked forehead and love songs whispered in the hush of her heart blown in from no where and no place as every face was the face of her lover.

I scribbled my story onto the page and I stared at the symbols looking for meaning I wrote some more ...with darker ink... and desperately looked for meanings ...for patterns
The more I wrote... the more confused I got... and the darker the page I started to look for an eraser... When I saw my story as a beautiful fairy tale... a flowing thought dream whirling around an imaginary I.... It erased itself and left a beautiful echo.
Knowing it is the dance is the dance. Everything's included and there are no things. Some laugh, some weep, some are the songsters, some are quiet. Some prefer to watch the sunrise, others the fire quench itself in the sea. Still others find themselves on the banks of a shoreless ocean smitten with the knowing and loving of life's fluidity.

You wanted to gather up life and put it in a seashell, to put it to your heart and listen to the universe breathing out breathing in. Deeply passionately life kisses you full on the mouth and you find yourself as love's desire. Bursting continually in this fire that moves my feet and moves this thumb across the glass, and floods the desert with tears.
Is it love or joy or wonder or simply the unspeakable beauty that we are that this is?
How deep the sky?
How fast the winds that sing in my heart?
How to measure this love?
Where is the end or beginning to the dream?
How wide how high how deep the dream of we are?

Looking for emptiness in the moonlight
You find only buckets of echoes
Under the cottonwoods
Wind rustles the shadows

In the darkest night your heart is pierced with brightness
Blood streams from that thorny kiss and you bleed into everywhere and no where
Release of what never was splashes like whiskered knives slashing your dreams of tomorrow

Deep down you've always known this
It has haunted you like a kiss in the night
As you stare into the fire of your own demise it pushes you
It is your own love calling you home

Time flows through you like an empty tide and leaves the memory
of love dissipating into a sea of dreams. All your beautiful footprints
wash away in the waves... they were never going anywhere
anyway.

Tongue lips teeth hearts gut
Mountain night
Crickets sing
Love sings
But only we know the words

We have never been anything other than these smiles these tears
these thoughts of moonlight raining
Sending love letters to ourselves caught in whirlpools of moonlight
For a brief moment
We flow through each other

I am this ever emerging un-capture-able immediacy, always
beginning always ending, never beginning never ending, just as it
seems to appear, never having any actual solidity or substance.
Painted by winged waves of whispers caressing the winds that soar
through me in me as me. Vast beyond ideas of infinity, more
intimate than love, supreme in its unknowability, leaving a hush a
silence a wake of marvel as time collides with eternity.

It's like a pure clear tone flows through you and erupts into an
unbound unrehearsed symphony, and the note fills you as it creates
you, and you are not separate from the song as it sings you and the
universe into existence. The beautiful illusion, the magic show of
separation, writing and unwriting itself simultaneously. Once seen
through this illusion of separation, this misconception created by

belief in words, there is no going back ...there is no back. The blinders will not fit. There is no one to wear them. Yet we never forget the pain, even as we are overwhelmed breathless blown away by the magic.

It's like you've lain down on the grass and the night sky crushes you and a warm summers breeze caresses you and you fall into the stars.

What if this were it, coyote? No bigger mind no higher or expanded consciousness. No god or true self or enlightenment. No future. Simply amazingly this aware-ing aware of aware-ing. Life touching feeling itself through you. A temporary window that cannot see itself or grasp what's going on, as it is what is going on. All ideas about what's going on are beautiful confabulations. Naturally occurring descriptions that create this universe of separate things and events that is the only world you can ever know. Knowing this is it and that it cannot be grasped as you are not separate from it, you are shattered immeasurably by the beauty
your beauty

I can't imagine wanting to feel any differently than I seem to feel. I really can't even imagine trying to capture the feeling or isolate it, for it doesn't feel like I am separate from feeling or thought or this ever emerging flowing dreamscape called life.
Am I embracing life?
Is life embracing me?
A seamless dance that requires an imaginary two step to fall in love with itself, this infinitely faceted center-less jewel is far more intimate than these very words as you read them, deeper and more expansive than love. A wordless whispering heart song sings me and it's name is desire. Without it I am not. The sublime feeling of all rightness, of completeness, includes all and everything just as it seems to appear whatever it looks or feels like.

How many rainbows will you have to drink before your cup is filled?
How many rivers are crossed before the current washes you away?

How many steps are taken before it's seen there is no where to go? How much washing scrubbing cleaning purifying will it take before you see yourself as perfect a jewel beyond measure?

This liquid gaze of infinity melts you into the seamless horizon, and your your tears are wrapped in sunsets as you dance the skeleton dance of fools. The beauty pulls you in and ravishes your heart out so you can re appear, looking …at yourself …smiling and weeping …from everywhere and no where.

It seems like you're entering the flowing, cloud reflections your only clothes slide off your nakedness as perfection subsumes you. But you had never left. It was only endless sky that beguiled your shadow until it danced into the sun.

Wandering on the shifting sands, your footprints dissolved as clouds swallowed the moon. Trying to catch the light in your hand as it slipped out of hiding, you stumble and fall, as up and down lose their solidity. Sea and sky become a mirror of your infinite beauty, there is no place you can turn away from yourself. Wonder swallows you whole.
Ideas of value versus valueless become meaningless, as meaningless slides into the vastness.

A wind song, a story-less story, we know it deeply and abandon the pen as ink stains become clouds and mountains. We disappear into seamless sky. The current, once begun, swallows itself, reappearing in various hues, aching to paint itself.
Rhyme and reason disappear, yet the singing continues. How wondrously the traceless wakes are hidden in splashing sky!
Oh! …countless poems are lost, the swirling gathers itself together, takes a breath, and is interrupted, and tree tops sings a constant show of shine and shadow telling the story less story of wind and sun.

and you have always been utterly alone, but in the dream oh the dream where love and beauty live and flourish,… I love you I love you I love you

Doves seem to like the peas we put in the feeder, and goldfinches appear to prefer the thistle seeds, and I love to watch these words silently appear on the glass screen, my thumb sliding across the smooth glass. How magnificent the dream paints itself with these thoughts these very words as we read them together, always new, yet made of memories, for how could we know a bird as a bird without the learned concept of bird-ness, how could we know the sun is warm without the concepts of warmth and coolness?
Yet there is an intuited knowing that these isolated things created by the lasso of words are made up, that they arise only in this thought dream that sings me and you and love and beauty into a universe where we are born and live and love and perish. We all know this amazing aliveness that seems to magically appear, looking and feeling like anything at all.

This flowing water color thought dream streaming across the mind screen bleeds into a mesmerizing picture show where no edges are actually ever found, no things or non things that are fixed or solid, yet it may feel like there is a kernel or a core that is unchanging. It may feel that there is a nothingness or even emptiness that is unchanging. Yet is there anything separate really? A separate thing called nothing? It can be recognized that this magnificent fluidity of life paints itself, water coloring on a river. This feeling is so beautiful, that all separation is imaginary, for how could there be beauty if there were no things to be beautiful or not beautiful?

Somehow it all feels beautiful to this imaginary dancer of winds.
Somehow it all feels like love to this pirouette of light.
Somehow the dream looks and feels like utter complete magic, to this center-less jewel that looks out from nowhere and everywhere, illumined by nothing, by everything.
The fallen plum leaf caught in the spider webs in the ivy, the desiccated butterfly, her delicate wings still shimmering in the morning sun.
This life, this life, this tender life that lives itself breathing touching dancing kissing itself through these lips that sing me sing you sing this song beyond freedom or non freedom as there is no one left to be free. Yet I am here simultaneously living and loving, dancing on the edge of a feather between the worded world and knowing and

feeling this great empty vast immeasurable unknowing that simply leaves me breathless.

Even unknowing and meaninglessness unravel until the unraveling unravels. I love your heart song that paints your beautiful story. Here I am, the story singing me, as without a song there is simply wordless unspeakable wonder. People say, 'I love you' or 'you're beautiful', and there is simply nothing here. Only in the dance with others do I find myself reaching out and grasping and kissing your beautiful hand. I am dissolved as this seamless primordial ocean without harbor or island... fathomless unknowable spaciousness, as love and beauty and awe swoon into themselves...
Is this bliss?
It has no name or shadow yet it becomes my transparent iridescence swirling... winged waves unfurl as sky dances through its own kiss and I am the taste of endless vast blue... I love desire. It kisses me into the dance.

As the ghostly captain of the phantom ship begins to dissolve into transparency it melts into the shoreless ocean. A dangling anchor may snag an old map or the prow may nudge an island of expectations or be lured by a mirage of certitude. The fortress of fear slams shut and keeps the hands clutching handholds that may solidify, perhaps until the day the seeker dies and realizes that he has been falling along with his dream handholds all along. No one has been inside the fortress or steering the ship. It was a sea of dreams. All along he had been the big wow. Awareness aware of being aware through this unbearably unutterably magnificent dream, this brief window of life catching a glimpse of its own sublime majesty and mystery.

I spent my whole life trying to decipher the code that would unlock the key to happiness. Looking for a key, I just knew had to be here. I could smell it! Forever running, trying to capture a dream.
Oh! to find the meaning of a cloud ....to grab the wind and sail away…
This, that seems to appear, of itself so, is unlike anything at all. Life is only like itself. The taste of tea, a symphony of perception, the

heat, the sense of liquidity, the sight the cup in your hand the steam... rising unfurling in the morning sun, your breath, how you get some spit ready to buffer the hotness, thoughts and emotions running, the feeling of your butt in the chair, leaf shadows dancing with the long morning light and reflecting on the shiny table, the smell of toast. I could write a book and take a picture and send you a tea bag in the mail...

Life... ahhhh..... so wonderfully un-capture-able ......simply wow

Not even a wisp of an ancient melody can penetrate what has no sides nor center and capture its own sublime beauty. Tendrils of love's memories weave this song of life that sings you sings me sings this sunlight caressing your tender face. Warmth and the coolness of the breezes of early autumn that catch falling leaves and dance this rippling memory through your mind stream.

Life does itself and breathes a descriptive world a dream that no one can understand or capture as we are this ballet of wind and sun and beauty. How beautiful that we cannot see ourselves or know anything or nothing. Yet we know deeply this life as it kisses itself sings itself through our lips our hearts our breath our song.

Knowing there is not even nothing underneath the story, and that there is no one to have one, is the story of enlightenment.

....a wisp of my hair moves in even the slightest breeze... a beautiful light sparkles in your eyes... one glimpse of the unlined world ...will make your heart sing songs more tender and beautiful than you could have ever dreamed... your heart song grows into such a fury, an ache you can no longer ignore... you will give anything to hear it again.

You will try to give up everything, but you cannot, as you are these things... Every goal, every heart's desire, all that you know, all that you care about, all that love, all that you were trying to hold onto... this terror of feeling so deeply, afraid of losing what was never yours.

Crushed by the enormity of what has no meaning nor direction, looking for answers ends. Pierced by loves heart magic your heart drops and love bleeds into the dream.

Her fear slid off and she glowed in the dark.
Wind found her sails and cupped moonlight into the dream.
Slipping through the words she lost the key and the lock and the door.
Hello swam through good bye and left wake-less ripples sliding to the edgeless edges where every dream died.
Neither up nor down, the finding of lostness lost itself in the vastness. Utterly ambiguous seamless emptiness filling her emptying her ...there is no edge or handhold and no one to grasp nothing. Wonder abounds when the grasping falls through itself. It was perfectly clear that she never had to get anything or go anywhere.

The hands were empty the pockets turned themselves inside out and beauty revealed itself. Naked Unadorned Breathless with your own magnificence. Songs of awe swim through the emptiness and spiral into themselves in chords that reverberate into a shimmer of your reflection... a gossamer light gown swirling caressing unowned unsigned emotion formless echoes dance and swirl in patternless patterns .....colors and shapes begin to form .....a tear emerges out of the inky blackness and catches its own reflection and sighs and smiles at its unadorned beauty.

Ahhhhhhhh........ tears splashing caressing all and everything touching you with your smile. Twirling in utter delight out of and into nothing, the world and all things are spun into existence ....a marvelous web of jewels ....and the most marvelous gem of all emerges…You.

This Bird Sings

The self, like a canvass stretched across the horizon, like a wall of
fear keeping out the sun, and the simultaneous knowing of the
inevitable sunset.
The paint may crack and crumble and light begin to shine... in you as
you through you... laughing and weeping madly as the horizon falls
into sky into sea, into itself, where never and forever collide... it was
a beautiful water color dreamscape flowing on a river, a magical idea
that there was someone holding the paint brush, and a pot of gold at
the end of the rainbow of fleeting... colors... that bled into this song
of wordless wonder that sings like this...
this sumptuous sensuous aliveness that has no words yet includes
all of them, that has no things, yet includes all things, that has no
wonder, yet wonder is found
everywhere
no where
here
yet not
this bird sings

Where did you get all these words concepts ideas that flow through
your mind stream? Is it YOUR mind stream? Obviously this flow of
thought does not go where you want it to. Obviously this flow of
feeling does not flow as you would wish. Can you find the beginning
and end to a thought or feeling or moment? Are there indeed
separate thoughts feelings or moments?
There would have to be a you outside of all this to find separate
thoughts and feelings and moments, wouldn't there...
...to gather time and plant a sunrise...

where are the edges to your heart?
what is this ache for the un-nameable
this beauty we feel yet cannot capture?
the wholeness the fullness this emptiness that shimmers so?
this sonorous silence that ripples its tenderness on your face?
is it your song?

this song of wind
did it kiss your cheek
as it dried your tears late last night when the moon was swallowed in wonder?
is the wetness, the dryness, the moonlight dancing in you or outside of you?
are there sides?
can you find a space between your cheek and the wind's kiss?
between a kiss and your lips?
between a breath and the song?
when is the dancer not the dance?
when is the singer not the song?

perhaps it is the not knowing that is so beautiful...
...are you separate from this beauty of unknowing?

If ya can't catch what's going on it's because yer not separate from it.
There simply is no now
Nor anyone to be in or out of it.

There is no outside to what's going on
And no inside...

Spring rains
Seasons flowing
Unbound treasure
How I used to long for the first robin song

This is it
She whispered
There is no that
Nor this...

This broken hearted beauty
Paints our silhouette with sky in sky...
The paint falls off the glass and the
Transparency of even love shines through

Sky just as vast and un-graspable in the night time dream
Lit from within

Lit from without
The moon shines
Not from the sun
But in your eyes

Through these eyes of aliveness
That no one wears
Brilliant searing transparency
Illuminates our reflection
Through each other's eyes

Liquid eyes of fire
Looking through this lens of love
Dissolving into our own desire
Chrysanthemum clouds billow and weep
We watch ourselves blown away
Ashes in the wind

….Not even his own tears held the wetness he longed for…

I have tasted your heart
It is mine as well
Beautiful all encompassing radiance
Like love
Like sorrow
Like awe
Like nothing at all
This searing brilliance
Burns even its own fire

There is no one to need meaning. No separate pieces to try to fit
together into a story of a timeline with a future. Even the ideas of
meaning versus meaninglessness evaporate. Stunning that that
which creates the illusion of separation which is so painful Is the

very thing which illuminates the world and itself. We are each other's words, each other's tears… unsigned poems….

There is a primeval language that has always been known …..yet we didn't know how to listen.
Trying so hard to grasp the silence… it's all the love you've always wanted and feared to lose. It's life full on unadorned. Realer than real. Utterly intimate naked utterly honest this life unowned is rich lush beyond belief. The center of I am loses its grip and spreads out to encompass …all and everything …the universe flows through you …. and you flow as the universe ….and the moon lights your nakedness like a infinitely petaled flower

The feeling that you have it …is it…
The feeling that you don't have it …is it…
The feeling like you've lost it …is it…
Or had it
Or need it
Or want it
Or don't want it
Or can do something to get it
Or can't do something to get it
Or feeling like you're searching for it
Or not feeling like you're searching for it… ….is it…
What could possibly not …be it?
You can't relax into or accept or surrender to that which you already are

We are our stories, this river of memories that whirlpool and swoop and tumble and create flowing pictures of things that seem to be stable when believed in, in time …a razors edge between birth and death…
Where is this silence?
What is its color, its shape?
Can we gather its golden leaves and the wind that tosses them in its flowing pirouette? Can we press this song into our hearts until the the story itself unravels its mystery?
Can we gather the flowers of last spring and toss them into the baskets of time?

When will the curtain of knowing part and reveal the gem whose shimmering incantations have beguiled and beckoned us since we emerged into this false front, this passion play, this bejeweled garment of understanding?
Where are the wings of life where do they not soar?
What is this vastness of death, and its certitude, that fills me with a beautiful silent melancholy of life's majesty?

'Where are my feet?' you no longer ask, as you fall into the dance you never left. The dance gazes onto itself through your eyes. Your heart dropped and sailed into the vastness imbuing every glance with your smile. Your touch magically touching itself.
Tears are your footprints.

It's like you're reading a long book, and you're deeply enthralled with the story, and you're waiting to see what happens next... Suddenly it doesn't make sense, it's topsy turvey... You notice the pages are no longer in sequence!
Some have been bound upside down and others, the text has been cut off mid sentence... The plot is lost the characters have forgotten their way ...or even that there was a path ...the treasure has sunk to the bottom of the ocean. The dragon eats the protagonist and all hope is lost.... and all fear ....and out of utter despair... something unspeakable happens.... the story is unraveled to reveal.....
That this, life just as it is, is the immeasurable treasure you longed for.

Dark and cold, mountain winds rush down the canyon, the morning sleeps, cat on my lap, steam rises. Leaves swirl on the surface reflecting eons of universes in a ripple that never was. Rich and lush, life, when time dies, there is a stillness, an unutterable silence. The hum vibrates your very being with a constant stream of all rightness. Knowing there is no other, it is never looked for. It was only a misconception that we could carry the sun through the night and fling it into the sky when we wanted to awaken.
In the hush of the great forest he found his heart, yet it was no longer his. Rudderless, adrift on a shoreless sea, sun slides across the vault of the sky, dolphins slip through the blueness and the orang-y reds of sunset ever linger in the sails calling you home. It is

a profound bittersweetness this unowned life, inside out our hearts unleashed, tears uncounted unlabeled the wetness the liquidity, the ache for simply this. A center-less wave welcomes you falling always into your hello, your own loving embrace your own kiss, emerging submerging folding into itself yourself your love, all love...

Fireflies hover, lanterns at sea, cast a wonderment of light and shadow that promise a shelter, a magic show of tomorrows to hold. Life sings and opens an empty hand. It beckons you to dance and you long to waltz into the shimmering.
Desire filled these paper sails and my origami heart collided into the tempest of dreams where forever crashed into never. Unfolding into reflections of tattered sunsets as river poured through its own wetness. Wet in wet in wet... river of dreams sings like this.

We exist only as this web of concepts. Like a rippling shadowland ....reflected watercolor dreamscapes flowing over and under and into and through the rippling of unheard untouched unseen melodies felt deeply yet never captured.
A cats cradle of self referential memories, thoughts, ideas swirling around an imaginary center.
Like ladders build of gossamer threads of moonbeams they can never be climbed.
Nor the moon ever captured.
All we can ever know is the reflection of moonlight rippling on the stream.
In wall-less canyons echoes emerge without sound, yet this heartbeat of existence is felt, this undeniable aliveness.
All trying to capture it seems to slice the sky into a gazillion pieces. And how could one piece of blue ever try to connect itself to sky when it has never been separate from it?

Windows crashed open into the heart of solitude. Love ripped off its skin and light soared through my heartache and swept my steps of loneliness into the rhythm of the night, echoing without end on the darkened streets. Forever and never began to kiss and I recognized their empty footprints.

Swinging from clouds that lost their imaginary tether to the sky, all encompassing edgeless wordless wonder sighs and falls though its own sigh, eclipsing the sun of tomorrows.

Loves wings soar through rippling shadows waving hello good bye hello, feathers as wide as life, as soft as death. Swooning into and through itself life weaves a dancing shadow that blooms into infinite petals and withers simultaneously, gems of wetness reflecting these tendrils of transparent tears flowing like this.

This bejeweled garment's beauty is that there is no one who wears it.

Self is a web of beliefs and preferences that weave themselves into a net that seem to capture an edge of sorrow that seems to hide joy. When it's recognized that under your beautiful bejeweled garment there is not even nothing, It's utterly breathtaking. It's like the universe soaring through you as you soar through it. A flowing light gown of awe swirling around an empty center. Wet in wet in wet in wet …tears fall like rain and leave no sign. They whisper my name in the echo of sea shells abandoned by the wind.

Wetness is its own reply.

I flung myself at the darkening sky desperate to drink another drop of light, and all that I knew and all that I cared for was swallowed in darkness. Even my desperation, which was me, swallowed itself in the deepening dream.

In the furrows plowed by hope and fear lay seeds of what I knew not, of emptiness, of wholeness, of a far off vast unknown unheard of radiance, where tiger lilies and fireflies wove bejeweled seamless songs over the edges of rainbows, where needles pierced the darkness, and magical light appeared, falling into starlight softly, and a whisper of nothingness sang a song of being, tripping the light switch into the ever emerging dawn. A brilliance I had missed, as I had been overwhelmed by my shadow, but had always been on.

Ever flowing unnamed tears washed rainbows through me in me of me as me, the universe glowing radiantly as itself.. When you finally tire of reaching for the sun, your entire world crashes, the light explodes and implodes into and through itself, and out of utter darkness the tips of your being feel a kiss that deepens until it consumes the very fiber of your being.

Light and warmth flood the edgeless edges of your heart, it is your own lips, your own breath, your own love. You are the flower the sun and the beauty pouring into yourself, washed away by your own tears into unspeakable awe.

Just as streetlights seem to reflect a dream world caught in a puddle, a pool upon the sidewalk, and crickets seem to dance and swirl a song that ripples through the night, like life like love like tenderness like sadness like every word that seems to touch the dream, it writes itself, and a multicolored bejeweled world emerges out of nothing where you dance.

Where you sing where you love, where your life happens utterly magnificently and uniquely in this temporary spotlight. An unbrushed unfinished canvass paints itself with infinite ephemeral colors like a soft caress upon your cheek, in a dream, in this dream that you are.

The tightness slipped off her shoulders and emptiness swooned at its own beauty. Dancing winds combed her hair and her song rained sparkling tears. Words formed themselves in the inky blackness and burst into bloom creating petals of wonder at their own delight and echoed back through themselves, diving again, leaving only a ripple of loveliness that pulled at a lover's heart string. Singing these very words painting the dream that paints me.

The song settles down into the song, heading into the sunset. Orbs of fire stream across the vault of edgeless sky, rainbows on my right, canyons on my left. A glance a kiss a touch of aliveness dances, hope and fear left behind, simply a vast expanse leaving not a ripple or a sigh…

Sourceless shadows dance weaving an imaginary web that creates you, that holds you in the middle of a dream. Spiraling outwards from nothing, tendrils of emptiness form illusions of color and form. Out of these imaginary lines painting imaginary moments time arises with a purpose, with a meaning, with a story that is you. Here you are, a trapeze artist on a timeline between birth and death, dancing through, in, as, and of a web, of yourself. Every arabesque seems to pause and be held for a moment and seems to surround and create and define the space around you, and within you. A magical illusion, like a real dream, inescapable, indivisible unutterably wondrous! Welcome to the world of separation, painted by learned shared words thoughts ideas and abstractions
The only place you exist

light pouring into light, space pouring into light, being in love and being love, dancing and being the dance itself, I am the song and the singer, the pure tone, the overtones, the reverberations, the echoes, and the vast vast silence, the poem writing itself on ripples as it erases itself, and the simultaneous knowing of the wordless words erupting constantly in unutterable awe, twirling in utter delight of delight itself, amazed at amazement itself, this life this life this life this life… we are not separate from it, it is what we are

storms rage, winds howling, diamonds falling, light splashing, inconceivable smoothness embraces all and everything, before and after only a dream, and up ahead, formless openness
a familiar ease and warmth wraps you folds you into itself your own breath your own voice welcomes you home, and every tear smiles

Words slide off the mirror as you crash through and shards of your brokenness dissolve into a blinding reflection of your beautiful edgeless heart. Memories paint the looking glass streaming colors, washing away the lines as they expose their fragile beauty. We can't see ourselves or one another without our imaginary lines. Knowing they are imaginary feels like love. A constant union of what was never apart. This all consuming closeness ignites and burns the distance between you and all ideas of love. In love as love through love, the dance is the dancer, and no where cannot be found.

Resistance formed her lines, strung like telephone wires in infinite blue. Ashes of love's memories tracked the edges of her footless steps, and blew away with the brilliance of her fortress dissolving into this magnificent immediacy.
Wind dances in the wake of its own unspeakable beauty.

Leaves fall like abandoned dreams
Webs untangle where hope and fear used to reside
Ashes ashes ashes
Flung into the night like stardust swirling on the dance floor of sky
There are no corners where they can gather
All your pockets have been unfurled
The softest breath sighs into its own sigh
Imaginary lines disappear
There are no words and yet we sing
There's nothing to say really
But I love you seems to work just fine

Walking in the canyon in the rain
Swooning into and through everyone I pass
So many beautiful beautiful eyes
Everyone a precious gem beyond measure
Can they sense this immense majesty of who they are?

Center-less placeless supreme vast spaciousness
A tiny window
A shimmering reflection
An imaginary aperture between inside and outside
Between the unknowable knower and the vast unknown unknowable
Like the surface tension on the soap bubble, the space inside and outside is the same. When separation is no longer believed in, the iridescent swirling is simply magnificent beyond measure!

Oh! The absolute rush of reality!
Sweet love songs echoing in the canyon...

They fall softly into the night and blend with the memory of all unwritten shadows dancing on the canyon walls.
I reach out my hand.. and grasp nothing, everything, even emptiness slips through my fingers. My hand itself dissolved, and the pure joy of never catching anything soothes the waves of the greatest tempest. I slip into light itself, as light.

Shadows play upon the surface of the water, diamonds of shimmering light sparkle on the waves. I look up and the stars carry me into the vault of the sky, the moon begins to peek over the canyon wall...
Midnight winds ease down the canyon, teasing a loose shutter. It's song everyone recognizes but no one can follow. A heartbeat without rhythm or rhyme, an ache of a memory bleeds into the vastness.
A shadow dances.
There are not even bones that rattle.

He held his heart in the palm of his hand, marveling, blown away by the beauty. His fear his terror like glue, like varnish, like oil on a beautiful bud. His petals ached to unfold, to lose themselves in the summer breezes, to bask in the mourning sun.
He was the clenching and the longing to release, and the longing to be held.
Unrestricted unformed spaciousness pulled him towards the edge where love cried out his name.
His echo danced and swirled and read his unspoken love songs of love lost and found. Kisses shimmering on empty winds moved him beyond joy and sorrow.
Pulled him under the wave of longing for more or better…
He fell into and through himself
We saw him one night
Dancing in the moonlight
On an empty beach
Humming a song no one could remember or forget

Trying to reach the end of desire, forever reaching for the gold ring, like trying to make angels in the grass. All that I'd heard about and all that I'd longed for, all learned ideas. I had learned about peacefulness so I try to be peaceful. I had learned about love so I tried to be loving. Looking searching seeking desperately for completeness for a place to rest for something I could hold onto. So I could take a breath and relax, to reach the end of desire.

The circle completes itself, the collapsing collapses, desire finds only desire, and all that I had longed for and all of my suffering and all of my pain was suddenly no longer mine. Every dream and every hope and every castle in the air and every place beyond the rainbow and every gold treasure hidden deep within the sea, every finger reaching out every thought desperately trying to grab hold of.... this magnificent un-touchableness.... all that trying that reaching for an idea for something else for something that wasn't present seemed to solidify the me. The searching the longing the neediness for what was not so. So exhausting, so painful, to believe in this illusion of separation.

Did you count your tears as you fell into midnight?
Did the wetness sink your saturated heart?
Have you gazed upon the dawn in utter wonder, and wished that the sunrise would never stop?
Have you followed the scent of your own aliveness looking for a tale of mountains falling into edgeless seas?
Running away from your beautiful humanness, trying to tear open the dream of bliss…

Fire burns, wind blows, tears fall, life flows. There is nothing outside of life doing it, it does itself. The dance dances itself the song sings itself, the painting paints itself, this passion play writes itself on the wind with wind, and it all blows away as it is written.
How many moments in a dream?
What is the taste of tasting?
How many moonbeams will fill your cup to overflowing?
Where is the end of sadness?
How many colors in the song of midnight?
How many tears in this empty cup
How many words to capture sky…

Truly it seems all seekers are trying to escape the dream. To escape the pain of feeling separate. I know that pain it was a constant presence in my life for almost 50 years. And my heart weeps. And my heart weeps. And my heart weeps. I just want to grab them and hold them and love them, and say this is it this is it this is it, there's nothing other than this life as it seems to appear, whatever it looks or feels like. There is no higher consciousness or pure awareness or some enlightened state of being that you're going to attain. There is no next. There is simply no you separate from what is going on.
Ever ever ever ever.
There Is simply no you who can step outside of life and change it or manipulate it or add something to it or take something away from it. And all your trying and all your trying to not try simply perpetuates the painful illusion of separation that you're trying to escape.
But there's nothing you can do to stop trying because there is no you separate from the trying.
I love you I love you I love you.

Knowing that I am and you are and love is made up somehow makes life more intense more wild more free more beautiful more perfect than I could've ever wished for or imagined or dreamed of. The imaginary gap between this and that collapses. Between you and life, you and me.
Everywhere you turn Is like swooning into your own winged beauty. Butterfly kisses from everywhere and no where as inside and outside have no meaning and there is nothing left to divide, you find yourself saying unabashedly nakedly, 'I love you'.

How long ya gonna pretend that everything is ok?
How much longer are you gonna pretend that there is a future?
That things will work out somehow?
How long ya gonna pretend that life has meaning, that it doesn't hurt, and that you are not going to die?
All those paths you have been climbing up the mountain are really slippery slides down into the edgeless sea. There is no where to get, there is no place to hide your heart, there is no escape. This is it this is your life right now right here whatever it looks or feels like.

Everyone you love will die, you will be forgotten... this could be your last breath.

There is no recess there is no cave no corner no place you can hide from that which you long for and fear. There is no garment that can clothe you. There is no place you can hide. There is no emptiness where you can stash your heart.

Hands fall into the very breezes they are made of, without edges or corners there is no place left to hide, no place to hang your hat in sky, no points can touch their own tips, no lips can kiss themselves, the stream of desire melts itself as it burns into your beautiful iridescence, and the chill of midnight swells the stars with magnificent awe.

I live on the shores of this edgeless sea of dreams where forever crashes into never and fullness collides with emptiness, where you and I meet and swoon into and through each other in this kiss that kisses us. Where cats prowl nightly and miss the beauty of their own moon shadow. Waves rush into the rocks, and discarded shells are washed in and out, tumbling into their own magnificent whorls and swirls of ancient time that writes itself on your fingertips.

He spoke of sun's sorrow at losing the dawn, and wept in awe as it could not be captured. Neither light nor shadow nor you or me dance alone in this day dream, as fingers of sunset beckon your shadow to return. One brief glance of life tasting itself through your lips is a thunderbolt of love piercing your heart. And where did love beckon from, where was the desire that slaughtered you? Whose sharp teeth glimmered in the dark just so? It was always your love that you feared to feel so deeply, that you feared you would lose. It was never yours to gain or lose, just a love dance of one of two of many of none.

In the night he saw that he was merely a reflection in his own dream. Empty hands grasping to stuff moonlight into his pockets. His songs, meaningless words, attempts to touch what was not there. His pockets were empty, moonlight a dream. He could not remember what he thought he wanted for it seemed that this was all he ever wanted, including the knowing that another would never hear his song…

Life, a tone poem
slides through itself and seems to leave a residue of song
a breath of emptiness
astounding
an atemporal syncopation this dancing this whispering scream, these silence hearts beating in rhythmless rhythm, no reason or rhyme....
a contrapuntal love song echoing dreams that mirror forgotten words where love reminds us of our beauty
and glistening overtones dance and sparkle across endless seas where the sky is always kissing itself

Footprints in sky
Dance of wind
Blueness
Like putting your hand through a mirror.
Like grasping a sun beam.
Like wearing a rainbow.
Like a musical reed naturally sings in the wind.
Like milkweed seeds spontaneously fly and dance effortlessly with no concern for their destination.
Like a mountain brook ripples laughter as it tumbles down the hillside.
It's song echoing in the deepest canyons.
Carried on the wind songs fly effortlessly and are heard or not heard naturally, and do not care if they are heard.
Seeds are planted only if they find a foothold and have no concern about it at all.

Moonbeams are reflected as naturally as starlight in my eyes. Songs are heard effortlessly by delicate eardrums. Starlight is seen spontaneously by tender eyeballs. My belly rumbles and is perceived as equally as rolling thunder.

A heavy load easily falls when the ties holding it up are severed. You cannot shut off your ears. Your skin shivers in a cold wind. When songs are heard that evoke this effortless freedom... they may be heard, and just as easily not heard. Perhaps it may sound like a grating noise or perhaps it will sound like a song your heart has been aching to hear.

Discerning a song from the playing of breezes upon your beautiful ears is easy when you're ready to listen. You have no choice. You never did.

The trapdoor opens and there is no more ground to stand on, and no handholds to grasp... no words, no symbols by which we can grasp this seamlessness, and there is a beautiful quiet when there are no edges, nothing can ever be cut, the sharpness is gone.

And the leaves and the wind are one dance, effortlessly naturally simply so, without reason or rhyme, and completely without any compulsion to discover any meaning I dance as the leaves in the treetops.

Everywhere I look there is only this dance.

I cannot conceive of there being separate things that are somehow reacting to each other like random billiard balls, or that there is a plan, or a source, or a script or a place where it needs to arrive, and I sing of this unicity and I watch as others listen and put my song into boxes of already conceived ideas of what this is like

...and the wind continues to dance and swirl and blow down the canyon.

I do not advise people to question beliefs as that would perpetuate the painful illusion that there is someone separate from beliefs who has them, and the illusion of personal volition, a you separate and apart from what's going on who can manipulate it, and the illusion that there is something called truth.

I have a friend who was commenting on various injuries she had had and said it made no sense until she found out about karma.

Self is a hodge lodge of beliefs and preferences, and the illusion of self seems to grow more substantial as it acquires more and more beliefs. Hearing of more and different concepts, some are rejected if they don't 'fit' with others, and some sound right, don't they? All of these to try to make some 'sense' out of what's going on, to fit together the seemingly split up pieces of life into a place of rest or understanding, and substantiating the feeling of solidity.

As underneath the flow of thought there is often an unrecognized feeling of slipperiness, of the intuited knowing that life cannot be caught which clashes with all these beliefs that make it seem like it can.
For indeed life simply happens as it does without reason or non reason, of itself so, and looks and feels like anything at all.

What if it began to begin clearly apparent that all the stories your brain is singing are made up? ALL the stories, including this one?
Stories of Karma and past lives and stories about how you are not going to awaken in this lifetime because you are needed here.
Stories that there are other or more lifetimes?
Stories like the universe listens to you and knows if your desire for this or that is self centered or not and will only respond to certain ones?
Stories like you are not a self?
Stories like life is supposed to be or should be this way or that?
What if life happened all by itself and the stories that seem to describe it also happen all by themselves and are merely the chocolate frosting, candy sprinkles on an unfathomable edgeless sea.

What if these stories simply paint the dream scape of time and beauty and love and you and me?
What if even things like truth were known to be made up?
What if beauty and love were realized to be stories?
What if it were realized that this is and you are simply a dream time story land painting itself through your thought stream?
That what was going on was simply and most marvelously unknowable?
The feeling of being tethered would slip away when you realized there was no time line to balance or cross. No one to be free or bound.
Truly even this story I sing right now seems to give a tether a handhold a point of certainty,...

269

The edge of the known world is devastatingly ravishingly beautiful and it will eat you alive.

She was the grace, she was the swallowing, she was the echo in an empty room.
She was the sunrise and the light upon her face, she was the kiss of midnight. She was the lostness she was the found-ness.
Nothing ever did anything, nothing ever did not do anything. There was no nothing. Her pockets were empty and disappeared.
She is an empty smile weeping.
A memory a hum a song of what never was. It was only the tweaking of imaginary lines that stayed her course, that trimmed her sales, and let the wind blow through her and move her.
You are the treasure, a string of pearls collapsing into itself.

Your heart cries out and you realize it was never yours.
They were never your tears they were never your rainbows, it was never your sadness it was never your joy.

Words are paltry pointers like smoke signals in the dark, yet they are all we have, they are our love songs to each other. The stories write themselves, the songs sing themselves, the dance dances.
Wind blows.
Tears sparkle in the glistening moonlight.
He so loved the breeze, the wind upon his tear stained cheeks, like love letters in the dark.
A kiss of midnight.
He could not hold it.
It touched him.
He touched it.
They found each other in between the touch-less touch.
There are no lines between you and your tears, between you and your sorrow.
How would you ever find yourself if not for this aching heart?
Where are the edges of love?
Where is the end of sadness?
Who can capture joy?
Where would you put it if you could?

Whose tears whose smiles whose love, whose life, who's sunrise?
Whose words fall from my lips, whose kiss whose song Is dancing in the darkness?
How beautiful unowned treasure
The walls become transparent. These lips are unowned and yet we kiss.

Everything you wanted was just hearsay just an idea, creating the idea of its lack in this moment. There was never any lack, there was never anywhere to go, there was never anything to get to find to capture. A treasure you can never have, you can never capture, you can never hold, as you are it.
It has always been you
The hush of midnight never left.

Ever shifting leaf shadows play along the carpet, so beautiful their dance lightly tripling, a sunbeam catches a crystal and rainbows slide along effortlessly, all shifting color light and shadow. Unable to mark where one begins and another ends, the magnificence continually blows me away.

Lying in bed not sleeping listening to the soft breath of night, rubbing my eyes, the cat asking for some more food, talking with my friends on facebook, shuffling over to the sink, the sound of water filling the glass, the weight of the glass lifting as the cold wet goes down my throat, noticing the Christmas lights reflecting on the faucet, feeding the cat and petting her soft fur, and all the while the awe that anything is happening at all. All of it… simply amazing. It feels like a wonderland, soft, edgeless, like floating soaring through and as this flowing.

Sky swooped down and swallowed you in its blueness, and you are the clouds. Wind blows through you and you are the wind, and all of it, no matter its appearance, seems like your hearts desire. The beautiful heart ache you ran away from touches you grabs you and pierces you with your own tender love, a joyful sorrow a seamless scintillating light flowing into and through itself through your beautiful beautiful eyes.

Not even a name for love, this deep felt kiss of nothing and everything.
You are the wishing, and its shadow dancing.
The edge calls as the heaviness of desire outweighs the fear…
Sunlight dances in shadow, inseparable from sun, heat frolics in cold night air.
Fire dances, longing breathes you, consumes you with your own love.

There is a placeless place, a place with no moon where light falls through the hole in your heart and even your own footprints are swept away. There seemed to be an anchor that tied you to the ground. It was your love. Where is this crown that toppled so beautifully as jewels exploded into infinite starlight? Like all of your efforts that fell away, the tears are not counted, yet they remain. Where is a droplet of dew on this hot dry afternoon?
Only in the tears of your heart where wetness sings as you settle into the sunset breathing.

He longed to be more in the now, but could not find an edge, an end or beginning to it. He tried to align himself with reality but he could not find a space or line between him and what was going on. He wanted to expand his awareness, his consciousness, but he could not find an edge or an end of it, or something apart from it that could pull it or stretch it.

How could he make larger something which had no edges?
He longed to fall into edgeless-ness yet he could not find anything apart from him to fall into.
Every effort was thwarted, and every non-effort failed to bring him closer to what he thought he wanted. The treasure, the golden marvel, the jewel, supreme spaciousness began to swallow his ideas of nothing. and everything. Including him…

This sublime aloneness reaches out its hand. It's your hand.
Reaches out its heart. It's your heart.
Mirrored shimmering reflections dancing echoing a love dance that permeates, that subsumes the dream.

The adventure of falling in love with infinite facets of your own center-less jewel that spins and sings you and me and we into the swirling is the heartbeat of existence.
We exist only our imaginary lines. There are no others nor ourselves. Nor love.
It has always been your love. Your song echoing in the dark.
Belief in the dream is loneliness. Not believing is a sublime aloneness.
A wondrous ok-ness an awe permeates the dream and feels like a love dance. Marvelous, this love of feeling like one like two like many like none.
The dream crochets itself just like this.
Songs flow, painting gossamer hands that fall through the cat's cradle they are weaving.

Sometimes when what I sing of seems like it's starting to make sense, like you are beginning to understand it or get it, there's a sense of relief. The relief comes from the idea that self feels safe in it's feeling of understanding. However there are no separate things or ideas or concepts or non-things that can be put together into some kind of place of rest or understanding. And there is simply no you separate and apart from what's going on who can manipulate it or accept it or reject it or surrender to it or allow it or understand it, as it's not even in it.

What's going on has no edges, can you find it outside to it? If there is no outside then there is no inside. This is not an it nor a non-it. What could possibly not be a what?
So many teachers give people ideas of what they should or should not do to attain this elusive goal called enlightenment. All of these perpetuate the illusion that there is a self separate and apart from what's going on who can manipulate it, who can do or not do something or nothing. All of these make the seeker feel safe. That is why they are so popular! Yet this dance is beautiful as neither the teachers nor the seekers are the choosers of their thought feeling or action.

For truly no seeker really want this. Very few will settle for less than nothing. No one who has experienced this profound shift in perspective that occurs in the brain was exceedingly brave, none of us chose this.

Most seekers truly just want to feel a little more peace, a little more ease in the dream of separation. They feel fine with the feeling that they are going somewhere, that they will get something, this golden goodie called enlightenment. Perhaps all their friends are seekers and they have beautiful communities.

Some however may become acutely aware that all they have ever done or tried to not to do in their entire lives have really not brought them one step closer to this elusive goal this idea, they truly do not know what it is, and all the scaffolding they have been building to try to reach capture the sky may begin to come crumbling down.

All of these ideas about what enlightenment is, where did you get those ideas? All of your beliefs about what life is about what you are about what the world is like, ideas like truth and meaning, they are all learned and shared.

What would you be without all of these beliefs ideas and concepts? Is there truly someone who has these ideas and beliefs? Anything that you may come up with is just another learned idea or concept. All words are learned and shared.

Is there anything under this beautiful flowing garment of ideas and concepts?

The mind of this and that paints a pseudo reality, the dream of objectified separation. The brain is trying to understand a product of its own imagination, cutting up a clear blue sky into a gazillion pieces, and wondering why they are separate, why it doesn't feel right, and tries to put them back together. The imaginary pieces (one of which is you) are sharp and it hurts.

What's going on is like a flowing gestalt without any split or division or edge. It is not a bunch of things interconnected. That is as far as the razor of thought can go as intuited unicity is beyond belief or understanding.

Night pulls in and parks next to the storm, and it's only the lightning that reminds us that there are no stars tonight.
Feet scuffling on the neighboring path.

The tip of a cigarette glows.
The richness the lushness of this night, of every night, of this ever emerging ever dissolving momentary, this brilliant immediacy of this life of every life, like a ricochet a rippling, an echo of unknown unknowable openness, a brief glimpse, a small window....
a silent symphony... singing itself with rain.
Strings... of words circling around and through the edgeless-ness, highlighting smiles, illuminating this love.

The moon slides over the edge of the canyon and lights my path.
Tears drenched in sunrise flow through me.
Where are my footprints?
I cannot find them.
Where is yesterday's smile?
Why did I think there was, why did I ever desire anything other than this as it is?

Life becomes a flowing liquid love scape, a sensual cascade of infinite jewelry flowing in you through you as you.

How truly amazing how perception and the simultaneous inseparable recognition of it occur utterly naturally, without any effort or non effort!
How magnificent the thought stream seems to describe what's going on, with the perception of sight and sound and taste and touch and bodily sensation as it paints the dream, yet it also sometimes seems to describe and paint pictures of memories, of a dream past, and conjure pictures of a dream tomorrow! As well as judging and comparing all of these seemingly separate events, usually as helpful or harmful to the dream star of the show, you.

All we can ever know is what it seems like for us. The dream scape of this and that and apparent separate colors and apparent separate forms and apparent separate moments (time) does not exist until the thought dream of shared learned words paints it.
There is not even nothing under the dream of this and that created by the razor of thought.

When the thought stream ceases even for just a brief moment, all thingness and you disappear. You don't even know it has stopped until thought returns!

It can be intuited but not cognized or known conventionally that all this and that and all apparent separation is mentally fabricated, never captured with words or caught by reason or rhyme.
As this seamlessness is always the case, it need not and cannot be brought about anew. As you, an apparent dream character are part of this seamlessness who cannot step outside of it, cannot manipulate or accept or allow or reject or surrender to this amorphous ambiguous flow of what we call life. Calling it this life seems to make life a thing, with edges that can be grasped, and a make believe apparent center (you).
As this is ALWAYS what's going on whatever this looks or feels like, the feeling that you are going against or with the flow Is the flow.

There's not something inside us which loves so deeply, It is us.

The fabric of a kiss weaves itself into a rippling song sung in the headlights of love's reflection, dancing down the road in front of you, never captured, but always apparent. The longing to capture love to hold this preciousness of life compels you to follow your spinning shadow and makes it feel like there really is a center to the swirling, the momentum created by the urge to chase your own tale. Spinning ever outward and inward it feels like you are being ripped apart by this fruitless sorrowful story of looking for love. There was never a you nor a home to leave, there has never been a you to be separate, yet you long for a sublime union and it is the fear of your dissolution that seems to keep it away. For what would life be if no one made it happen? How would the wind blow if no one sang?

You watch your feet move on the sidewalk your shadow preceding you, the wind your breath. A kiss of midnight rains tears of despair, will you never find this elusive goal you have longed for your entire life? All ideas of peace love enlightenment washing away in this flood dissolving and filling and emptying the holes in your heart as it explodes.

Night flew in like the wings of an owl softly forcefully and you can not find yourself in the darkness and you are lost in the light.
Where were your tears in the rain?
Where was the meaning of wetness as your sorrow flooded into joy, into a heartache that pierced all ideas of love?
Where was the kiss you had always longed for? It finds you in the darkness, your own tenderness, your own lips, your own voice, your own breath, your heart your song your life revealed to be no ones.

You step out alone and naked into the light, knowing there is nothing under this utter nakedness. The dance and the dancer, the light and the reflection. The harmony the chorus of one of two of many of none.
Where was the beginning of time?
Where was the end of love's infinite kiss?
Where were the memories you had forgotten?
Where was that smile you glimpsed one night a million moons ago?
All of it and none of it swallowed in the embrace of the richness and lushness of this ever blooming ever wilting tenuous tender flowering of life kissing you singing you as you sing it.

Enlightenment is not being a someone who is disassociated from self or life. It is a total and complete shift in perspective that occurs in the brain when It is known and felt always that self and all thingness is made up, yet loving the appearances of selves and things. Many believe enlightenment is seeing through the illusion of self. However thingness also must be seen through The entire dream of separation is known to be mentally fabricated, yet it does not stop. It is like living between love and nothing at all, knowing that you and love are made up. There is a knowing feeling always, that there are no separate things, no separate events, no separate people. That all qualities and characteristics, time dimension causality, and all measurement is fabricated and composes the dream of objectified separation that is created or painted by the brain. Somehow the brain sees through its own charade, so to speak, and no more is it believed. Even non-belief is not believed. It has nothing to do with accepting or rejecting the self or life as it seems to appear.

Between what has never happened and what will never happen there is a lustrousness which omits eternity. Never and forever kissed and lost themselves in their own embrace. This river which has washed away your footfalls and swooned through your heart has swept away all the side eddies and merged with the tides of no tomorrows.
This meeting of time and timelessness leaves a hush in your heart after it has been plucked with the blooming and wilting beauty and sorrow of roses and thorns, and bled it's beauty into sunsets maw.

Tenderly the cat wanders among fallen leaves where you used to search for memories of fallen rainbow treasure. Now consumed by the silence that was simply missed, wind sings soaring leaves, and a forgotten timeline watches your hands dance through the loose ends of transparent light fabric, unweaving tattered memories of footfalls that fell through the dance.

In this trackless land there are no handholds, no center in pure vast spaciousness, no toeholds in these fathomless depths, no stars to follow, no edges to fall off, no place to rest or take shelter from an all consuming storm that leaves you breathless in its awe filled super complete utterly devastatingly beautiful enormity of infinite emptiness.
Extending everywhere and no where without time or direction inwardly and outwardly, without sides, piercing the very marrow of your being, more intimate than any feeling you have ever had, and any thought that ever seemed to trace your silhouette in the dark, or caressed your lips your kiss your smile your tears and plunged your heart into a wall of blackness and ravaged every notion of what life should be, what you should be, ripped apart all ideas of future and past and time itself, dying, it's embers catching the last rays of this sunset that has been beckoning you since you felt yourself to be alone and separate in a far away galaxy in an isolated universe in this place you had called your home your life, your longing for love.

dipping and swirling into and over and under and through each other, light in light pouring through light

this richness and lushness of life dancing as one as two as many
kissed caressed from the inside and out, this iridescent flow of
shadows blooming into a song of me of you of tender winds
dancing down the grand canyon of love
In love as love through love.
No you nor love

He was the ache of the evening
The song of the sidewalks
The dark encroaching
And the pool of light
He was the Nighthawk swooning and the sirens blazing
The hush of the evening and the hush before dawn
He was the song of the dancers in the empty bar hall
The crickets love song and the chorus of the sprinklers
Empty footsteps in the night
A gossamer light gown shimmering reflections
Intimate jewelry sing of day pouring into night
Mountain stream
Does not shimmer or sing
Without a listener
River needs its banks to flow
Love requires imaginary twoness
A dance of one in love with itself

Fragility and impermanence of flowers is their obvious beauty, their
tender delicate trembling jewel of life's joy and sorrow
Wall-less canyon echoes our love songs, always a new song,
created and destroyed simultaneously
I reach out to touch you and slip inside myself
The universe dances, unrehearsed, without reason or rhyme just
this dance that you are that I am that we are, twirling down the
grand canyon of love.

He had spent his entire life building a castle trying to reach the sky,
trying to capture the blueness. Without any warning the turrets
started to crumble as his dreams of more or better or future were

dashed. He saw that the lines between him and the sky were imaginary. There was nothing solid or stable or fixed, even love was an idea...
Until there was not even nothing left
it came as quite a shock that without an imaginary castle to live in without love, he could not find himself.

I didn't know what I wanted, I had vague ideas of peace, wholeness, love... just to stop chasing my tale, and in the end I couldn't pretend anymore that everything was ok.
Fighting against the darkness, believing that there had to be a key somewhere that would switch on the magic I just knew I was missing. It was a shocker to realize that none of these concepts were my own.
Even my name.
When deep seated beliefs began to shatter at first it was terrifying! What would I be without them? I had no idea about no self but I began to feel free-er and free-er.
All the problems of self improvement, ideas of perfection, of a time in the future when I could finally relax, of what life should be, slipped away.
When the assumption of personal autonomy evaporates all that effort-ing to constantly create maintain and defend an illusion stops. There is a total relaxing into as the vastness, like drifting down and as a warm stream utterly immersed subsumed as this sublime joy and wow-ness of simply being.
It was my own tears that rusted the hinge, the doors fell off, only transparent curtains raining through my mind.
A breath unowned un-captured, this simple touch of nothing caresses me. Ruby slippers are not necessary to find your way to what has always been the case.

It's like being the deep fathomless ocean, you look and see the waves on the surface rise up and shatter into multitudinous sparking drops reflecting oceans depths and ever un-reachable shores, and you are untouched, yet not separate from the water as it roils and boils, or yawns and sleeps. With every wave you say hello, with every crash of thunder on the shore you roar this lions dream. You are moved yet undisturbed.

Infinitely arrayed iridescent shards of midnight slay your very being until your heart drops and this sublime liquid crystalline matrix of this and that woven into a dream of utter beauty amplifies and breaks open the light, the unbearable magnificence once seen, grabs you and rakes you and shakes you apart at the seams and blows you away
slipping sliding beneath the waves of dignity, gone are the days when you were trying to squeeze life into what you thought it should be

He had been the questions, now they are gone. He had been hope and fear for the future, but time had died. He reached out his hand to brush away his regret for the past but could not find it. He had been the ache for meaning but no longer wished to find it. He had been the need the hope the fear the overwhelming desire to capture life to hold it to caress the treasure he felt so deeply, and all that was left was this.
This ungraspable jewel without a center this shimmering without meaning or non meaning, this atemporal flow without beginning or end, always beginning and always ending, oranges and reds of sunset always reflecting on the sails, death his constant companion. Waves of fullness sparkle and shimmer as they ripple into and through themselves crashing into the shores of a bottomless edge-less sea.

She had been reaching out to touch the magnificence, to pluck the flower, to learn the words to the dance, to swallow vast blueness, to fall into the sky, to hold her heart, to bask in the warmth the magic the life she felt was so fleeting so beautiful she could not bear the thought that it would end someday...
Every handhold crumbled and every footfall continued unplanned and every song sang itself without rehearsal. There was no ticket to the dance, no key to unlock the treasure, she had never needed to look for it, as it was the looking for at that seemed to hide it. She was the flower, she was the magic, the impermanence and un-graspability was it's very beauty
...and shine fell through shadow and only the dance remained

All maps are dream maps. Fingerless fingers pointing to placeless places.

He tried to erase himself but every move he made etched his shadow deeper into the street of time. Incising his name in his heart with shards of broken mirrors.

How could there be a path to wholeness to oneness? He noticed an ease when his thoughts were slow, yet night came whether he thought about it or not. Thought seemed to disrupt the flow and create waves and whirlpools and rip tides in the shimmering but oh! The reflections were so beautiful...

He tried to do nothing, and tried all kinds of ways to be free. But they all just drew the noose in tighter, until every step, every breath was an effort. Every heart beat was heavy, like a bubble in molasses he could no longer move nor not move.

Painted into a corner of his own desire there were no more footprints to follow.

He realized he had never done nor not done anything, ever, in his life.

He could trace his life in the water colored images as they floated across the screen, but it no longer felt like his life. It was like a movie of a dream. He had forgotten his lines, but he always knew what to say. He had forgotten his part, but it always seemed to play itself as it had always done.

The sun rose itself, and the moon captured his heart every evening, as it had never been his.

Effulgent transparent glimmering shining emptiness exploding imploding running down and into and through. Folding through itself, lost in its own spiral. No longer looking for an edge a tip an end or a beginning of a thread to pull, the tapestry weaves itself as it has always done.

It is the scent of nothing, the sent of freedom, the sense pervading all and everything, this undeniable aliveness that lets you know you are alive.

Without us there is no dance, without us there is no party, without imaginary twoness there is no knowing of our aliveness.

Phantoms dance and sing and swirl in the moonlight to tunes no one else can hear. Like a song they forgot and cannot remember, it aches somewhere deep in their hearts.
And the partygoers in their beautiful dresses slide down the sidewalk glimmering in the street lights. I want to touch them to hold them to dance with them to cry with them, to say, 'you are beautiful. I love you'

No invitation is required, there is no dance hall, there is only this dance, unrehearsed, every step is perfect. There is no more looking or wondering how to be, how to love, how to live, how to die. Wild eyed and naked there is no concern for what others think or believe.
Yet this dance needs two. A song requires a listener. Footsteps are empty when the dance floor falls away.
Sweetly salty, the taste of taste itself returns to the shoreless sea where all your dreams of love died
Peering out of an empty room sliding away in an avalanche of tears, It is this song that brought me back. My heart song your heart song, this heart song of love itself that sings us.

I thought I could let loose this love
But I am learning to step back
Like this ever present awe
It sings, still
These tears you may not notice
Illuminate my eyes

This slow sensuous waltz
Light and shadow
leaves trunks and branches
dance in their own sea of green
As dark mountain echoes
Pirouette with sun's embrace
One red flower by the path

This beauty loosed itself upon me
Slaughtered me with its ravishing intimacy
Pierced me with loves heart magic

Exploding and imploding into fathomless softness
Where all and everything is an arabesque of love.

I love you I love you I love you I sing
Earth and sky reflected in your vast eyes
Where seas drink this tempest of love

But I may just say
Hello
Or good morning
The rakes of your discomfort
Hurt me as well.

Just a mile in your shoes is a lifetime in my heart.

where were the clouds to hide his nakedness
and this piercing blue
where was the smile
to hide his tears
to hide
the bite
the hurt
he could no longer deny

the paint on the window was a most liquid blue
yet sky could never be captured with a tear

trying to quench his thirst with sunlight
it sucked into itself
dry as a bone
an empty shadow danced on the water
until he saw the tender ache of his own reflection
Weeping

There is no key
Nor lock
Nor door
To slide-less-ness

The wall of belief, when no longer believed, loses its glue of hope and fear and becomes transparent. Baseless brilliance shines through all and everything, knowing and feeling this edgeless seamlessness. Always knowing that all thingness is made up, including you! Some beliefs seem to fall away, some remain, yet none are believed. Nothing feels solid. The passion play has no real center. There is no more trying to find a source or understanding, to fill in the blanks as there is no equation that needs resolution, all feels complete in this delicious unknowing, suspended as vast ocean falling through sky.

The thought stream continues somewhat like before, yet it feels silent, like there is no one listening. You are alone as this silence... There is no one in, or behind the mirror.

He spied some empty footprints and was captivated by a melancholy essence of what he knew not. Lured by a memory of a scent of a goal of something to capture he followed them. He found his feet matched perfectly as they wandered together, apart, in the darkness, in the lonely desert, past the mirages where he knew there was nothing that could quench his thirst, past the caravans where colorful people danced and sang, trying to keep the darkness away.

He grew weary and began to wonder if it was the path he wanted, but he could not stop his tears as they began to fill the imprints, the sides began to crumble.
He saw his reflection in the dying light and realized he had been following himself. Looking for his own tale, his own love, his own embrace. His heart was pierced by his own song.
He looked back and could not find his footprints, and gazing ahead he could find no path. Looking down his shoes were empty. Looking up there was an memory of a shadow saturated with his reflection in sky.

Moonlight rushed through his nakedness and there was only the song of diamonds shimmering skimming the surface of a bottomless sea.

A shadow raced across the vastness. He looked up and never found the shape of darkness.
Light pouring into light, winds whispering songs of love, phantoms dancing, circling and swallowing the sun.

Drowned dissolved as the sea of edgeless beauty, my sourceless reflection soars over billowing ripples of love's sacred melody echoing the heartbeat of one of two of many of none.
Under this raiment of a poet's song, behind these liquid eyes of love, beneath this naked unadorned sky like wonder, there is not even nothing at all.

Made in the USA
San Bernardino, CA
15 September 2018